Cambridge Elements

Elements in Law, Economics and Politics

Series Editor in Chief
Carmine Guerriero, *University of Bologna*

Series Co-Editors
Alessandro Riboni, *École Polytechnique*
Jillian Grennan, *Duke University, Fuqua School of Business*
Petros Sekeris, *TBS Education*

CORRUPTION AND THE VOTER'S DECISION

Experimental Evidence from Brazil

Miguel F. P. de Figueiredo
University of Connecticut School of Law

CAMBRIDGE
UNIVERSITY PRESS

Shaftesbury Road, Cambridge CB2 8EA, United Kingdom

One Liberty Plaza, 20th Floor, New York, NY 10006, USA

477 Williamstown Road, Port Melbourne, VIC 3207, Australia

314–321, 3rd Floor, Plot 3, Splendor Forum, Jasola District Centre,
New Delhi – 110025, India

103 Penang Road, #05–06/07, Visioncrest Commercial, Singapore 238467

Cambridge University Press is part of Cambridge University Press & Assessment,
a department of the University of Cambridge.

We share the University's mission to contribute to society through the pursuit of
education, learning and research at the highest international levels of excellence.

www.cambridge.org
Information on this title: www.cambridge.org/9781009499743

DOI: 10.1017/9781009499736

First published 2024

A catalogue record for this publication is available from the British Library.

ISBN 978-1-009-49974-3 Hardback
ISBN 978-1-009-49976-7 Paperback
ISSN 2732-4931 (online)
ISSN 2732-4923 (print)

Corruption and the Voter's Decision

Experimental Evidence from Brazil

Elements in Law, Economics and Politics

DOI: 10.1017/9781009499736
First published online: December 2024

The co-editors in charge of this submission were Carmine Guerriero.

Miguel F. P. de Figueiredo
University of Connecticut School of Law

Author for correspondence: Miguel F. P. de Figueiredo,
miguel.defigueiredo@uconn.edu

Abstract: Despite voters' distaste for corruption, corrupt politicians frequently get reelected. This Element provides a framework for understanding when corrupt politicians are reelected. One unexplored source of electoral accountability is court rulings on candidate malfeasance, which are increasingly determining politicians' electoral prospects. The findings suggest that (1) low-income voters – in contrast to higher-income voters – are responsive to such rulings. Unlike earlier studies, we explore multiple trade-offs voters weigh when confronting corrupt candidates, including the candidate's party, policy positions, and personal attributes. The results also surprisingly show (2) low-income voters, like higher-income voters, weigh corruption allegations and policy positions similarly, and are slightly more responsive to candidate attributes. Moreover, irrespective of voter income, (3) party labels insulate candidates from corruption, and (4) candidate attributes like gender have little effect. The results have implications for when voters punish corrupt politicians, the success of anti-corruption campaigns, and the design and legitimacy of electoral institutions.

Keywords: corruption, voting behavior, elections, accountability, conjoint analysis, survey experiment, Brazil, and Latin America

JEL classifications: D72, D73, K4, K16

ISBNs: 9781009499743 (HB), 9781009499767 (PB), 9781009499736 (OC)
ISSNs: 2732-4931 (online), 2732-4923 (print)

Contents

1 Introduction

Politics and corruption are seemingly inseparable. In 2014, nearly one-third of the members of the Indian Parliament had criminal cases pending against them (Varghese, 2014). As of May 2016, in Brazil, 59 percent of Senators at the federal level either had convictions or had a criminal investigation in the past, and roughly the same proportion were in the same situation in Brazil's lower house (Smith, 2016). In Romania, more than one quarter of the country's forty-one mayors elected in the June 2016 election were either under investigation or placed under preventative arrest for corruption (Bucureasa, 2016). This phenomenon is not limited to developing countries; from 2009 until 2015, 16 New York state legislators had criminal convictions that included federal corruption, bribery, embezzlement, extortion, tax evasion, and perjury (Craig et al., 2016). More recently, in June 2024, within 24 hours of being convicted on 34 felony counts in a hush money trial, former U.S. President Donald Trump's campaign stated they raised $52.8 million. In all of these cases, polls showed high voter dissatisfaction with corruption, yet significant numbers of politicians with corruption allegations and convictions running against "clean" candidates got reelected.[1]

If corruption is strongly disfavored by voters, why do corrupt candidates remain popular and keep getting reelected? In addition, when do voters consider candidates for elected office to be corrupt? These questions are of great importance for a number of reasons. First, understanding how voters perceive candidate corruption can be predictive of electoral outcomes. When evaluating candidates accused of impropriety, success in the voting booth for these candidates can be determined by the norms that determine corruption. Second, having an empirical foundation for how the public perceives corruption can also serve as an important basis for designing interventions to change such norms and laws that govern the electoral process such as campaign finance reform and anti-corruption laws. Third, understanding regional differences in candidate perceptions of voters can lead toward building theories that explain variation in toleration of candidate corruption. Finally, uncovering divergence in how courts, laws, and the public define corruption has implications for the legitimacy of democratic institutions and electoral accountability.

One critical function of democracy is the power it gives to the citizenry to punish or reward politicians for their performance through elections. This form of vertical accountability provides an important check on those in power,

---

[1] Varghese (2014) states that a report by the Association for Democratic Reforms showed that in India "the chances of winning was higher for candidates with criminal cases, compared to the candidates with a clean record." Bucureasa (2016) states in a poll taken two months before the election, "more than 82 per cent of Romanian voters wouldn't cast their ballots for a person who is under investigation or on trial on corruption charges."

and is one important feature a number of scholars have stated is necessary for democracies to be self-enforcing and self-sustaining (Przeworski, 2003; Przeworski, Stokes, & Manin, 1999). Specifically, elections provide the authority to govern, while also determining "winners" and "losers" signaling to candidates what policies and behaviors should and should not be followed (Przeworski, 2003).

Yet, often, we see that corrupt politicians frequently get reelected, potentially undermining the promise of democratic accountability and the rule of law. Consider the following examples.

- *Alcee Hastings, former US District Judge for the Southern District of Florida and current US Representative for Florida:* Hastings kept getting reelected even though he is one of the only handful of lifetime appointed federal judges impeached by Congress for his role in a bribery scandal. The veteran Democrat was also embroiled in a number of scandals and has been ranked No. 1 out of 435 members of the US House for nepotism as the result of abuses as a federal lawmaker that allowed him to benefit himself and his family, mainly by paying his girlfriend and relatives salaries and fees. Hastings is also a member of Judicial Watch's corrupt politicians list. In the spring of 2011, Judicial Watch filed a lawsuit against Hastings on behalf of a female employee (Winsome Packer) who was repeatedly subjected to "unwelcome sexual advances, unwelcome touching" and retaliation when he chaired the United States Commission on Security and Cooperation in Europe. The suit, filed in the US District Court for the District of Columbia, led to a House Ethics Committee probe as well. Despite this history, the 72-year-old Hastings retained his seat by a wide margin.
- *William Jefferson, US Representative from Louisiana:* Jefferson earned the nickname "Dollar Bill" for stashing a $90,000 cash bribe in his freezer. He eventually was convicted of nearly a dozen corruption counts – including bribery, racketeering and money laundering – and was reelected after being indicted.
- *Paulo Maluf, current federal congressman in Brazil's lower house (Câmara dos Deputados), former governor of the State of São Paulo and former mayor of the City of São Paulo:* Maluf was indicted in New York, and has charges pending against him in Brazil for being part of a conspiracy to embezzle and conceal public funds. In addition to conspiracy, the indictment by the New York County District Attorney's Office also charged Maluf with grand larceny and criminal possession of stolen property.

All these cases involve the successful reelection of candidates who had been involved in clear cases of corruption, but they also vary in important ways.

The cases vary in the type of corruption in which the candidate is engaging. The actions include favoritism (nepotism), accepting bribes, embezzlement, and money laundering. They also vary in the extent to which the alleged act results in private enrichment versus advancing a campaign or policy preference of the candidate. Legal actions taken in response to the alleged corruption also differ. Beyond the corruption itself, candidate attributes, such as the individual's gender, race, party, and public office are all important factors that play into the candidate's reelection prospects. The candidate's links to voters, policy positions, and performance on the job are just some of the factors that influence the probability of reelection given a corruption allegation. Finally, in more extreme circumstances, anti-corruption activists and protests seeking to highlight the issue have encountered violence, repression, and divide-and-conquer tactics from governments or groups linked to those in power (Chayes, 2018; Dunning et al., 2019).

These countermeasures and other factors create information deficits that undermine democratic accountability. A long tradition of work in normative and formal political theory demonstrates how a well-informed electorate is critical to a highly performing democracy.[2] In standard principal-agent models, the electorate delegates governance and administrative responsibilities to elected politicians. But as Przeworski et al. (1999, p. 29) and Dunning et al. (2019, pp. 3–4) point out, the claim that representative democracy in the form of contested elections, widespread participation, and citizen liberties guarantees efficacious governance is problematic. In most cases, effective democratic governance emerges when voters are informed about politicians running for office so they can select candidates whose preferences align with their own, and who are qualified, competent, and trustworthy. At the same time, incumbents must realize their performance is subject to the public eye and that poor performance will result in electoral defeat (Dunning et al., 2019, p. 4). Effective transparency, information provision, participation, and engagement are all important ingredients in a well-functioning representative democracy with accountability that reduces the chances of empowering corrupt and/or incompetent politicians from assuming power.

We currently lack a coherent framework that explains the reelection of corrupt politicians. This study is partly focused on providing a framework for understanding the conditions under which voters will punish or reward

---

[2] Dunning et al. (2019, pp. 3–4) clearly articulate this point, where the authors cite a wealth of literature, including Pitkin (1967); Dahl (1973); Dahl (1989); Przeworski, Stokes, and Manin (1999); Brunetti and Weder (2003); Besley and Prat (2006); Malesky, Schuler, and Tran (2012); Bauhr and Grimes (2014).

corrupt politicians, and then testing aspects of the framework empirically. Although formal rules, well-designed laws, and efficient institutions are often important determinants of electoral accountability, they are often insufficient in curbing candidate corruption (de Sousa & Moriconi, 2013). In order to advance the discussion on what is sufficient, the next section examines the factors that determine how corruption is defined by voters, and what will lead them to reward or punish corrupt politicians in elections. The section that follows explores *when* voters will punish corrupt politicians by relying on a lab-in-the-field experiment to see if informing voters about the corruption of politicians will have a causal effect on their intention to vote. The section examines important trade-offs that voters make in evaluating candidate corruption by experimentally manipulating candidate attributes presented before voters. The results of this experiment shed light on the *mechanisms* that will lead to varied outcomes in voting behavior that ultimately answer the question of *why* voters punish or reward corrupt politicians.

The results show that party labels can insulate a politician from corruption allegations, even if the allegations involve private enrichment corruption. First, I find that voters are most likely to punish private enrichment corruption, rather than corruption that benefits their campaign, in contrast with theories that suggest that voters equate corruption across candidates and tend to privilege other dimensions. Second, I find that voters are responsive to candidate policy positions, although the effects are not as strong as their responsiveness to party labels. Finally, the candidate's gender neither helped nor harmed his or her probability of receiving a vote. Other attributes such as proven leadership ability and closeness to the people were borderline in terms of their chances of increasing the probability of the vote for a candidate, but high intellect had a stronger effect. Heterogeneous treatment effects show that low-income voters do not differ from middle- and high-income voters in the weighing of corruption allegations and candidate policy positions; low-income voters are responsive to court rulings on electoral corruption, and are only slightly more responsive to candidate attributes than middle- and high-income voters.

Although some of the existing literature posits that lower income voters are distinct in their responses to corruption from middle- and high-income voters (e.g. Almeida, 2008; Botero et al., 2015), I largely find that the two groups are similar, with the exception of how they react to court decisions on corruption. Specifically, I find that poor voters differ from their wealthier counterparts with respect to how they react to court rulings on electoral corruption. Middle- and high-income voters are largely unresponsive to court rulings and need a very strong negative signal from the courts (e.g. guilty in a trial court and on appeal) in order to increase the probability of punishing the candidate. Poor voters are responsive to court rulings, but primarily to guilty rulings; once a candidate is found guilty by a trial court, even if they are appealing or subsequently acquitted, the candidate has a higher likelihood of being punished and little correction is made after any conviction. Irrespective of income, the findings are consistent with distrust of signals of innocence from courts on electoral corruption, and with a view that guilty politicians engage in prolonging the process through appeals or purchase not guilty verdicts through hiring skilled defense lawyers. Unlike their counterparts with more income, with lower income voters the probability of not receiving a vote increases based on having the presence of a court conviction. This behavior is consistent with a belief that lower income voters might be predisposed to be more trusting of courts when they convict possibly because they are more deferential to state institutions, or the guilt of the politician is made more salient by the court's conviction, irrespective of when that conviction occurs.[3] Overall, the court rulings provide a stronger signal to poor voters that is likely to affect their vote choice. The result stands against work that finds that the poor equate corruption across candidates and respond to information in unsophisticated ways.

The conceptual and empirical work make a number of contributions to the existing literature. First, while there is a vast literature about the consequences of corruption, research on what leads government to change to being clean is still nascent. As Adserà, Boix, and Payne (2003, p. 446) succinctly state: "[i]n contrast to the mounting scholarly research on the consequences of good governance, our knowledge about what causes governments to be clean and efficient is still at its infancy." Though the authors made this statement about the state of the literature almost two decades ago, I would argue that the literature is still at a similar stage with respect to what leads governments to become clean.

Second, a theoretical and empirical literature focused on voting behavior posits that increased information given to voters will result in increased turnout (Feddersen & Pesendorfer, 1996; Palfrey & Poole, 1987). The hypothesis is also prominent in work that has focused on corruption. Treisman (2000), for instance, suggests that increased transparency in democracies reduces corruption. Similarly, Kunicova and Rose–Ackerman (2003) assume that when corruption is made public, a candidate's reelection prospects decrease. The empirical sections in this Element show that under certain conditions, increasing information can lower voter turnout, leading to the need to place scope conditions on such theories.

---

[3] One other unlikely possibility is that low-income voters are specifically distrustful of appellate courts, but I find this explanation unlikely.

Third, measuring the causal effect of corruption information on voting behavior is challenging, since information about the corruption of politicians is confounded by numerous other factors such as socioeconomic status and party identification. Much of the literature uses cross-national, descriptive survey and observational data to make model-based inferences about the effect of corruption information on voting behavior (McCann & Dominguez, 1998; Pereira, Melo, & Figueiredo, 2009; Peters & Welch, 1980; Welch & Hibbing, 1997). These studies make strong assumptions about unobserved factors being "controlled for" in the statistical model. A more recent literature relies on field and natural experiments to make stronger causal inferences about the effect of corruption information on voting behavior (Banerjee, Green, Green, & Pande, 2010; Banerjee, Kumar, Pande, & Su, 2010; Chong et al., 2015; de Figueiredo et al., 2023; Ferraz & Finan, 2008; Humphreys & Weinstein, 2012). A noteworthy recent effort to promote replication and standardization of field experiments across a variety of countries on information and democratic accountability is the Metaketa I Initiative, detailed in Dunning et al. (2019), where research teams working in a number of countries standardized a treatment arm and examined the effects on electoral behavior. Nevertheless, this area of research is still nascent, and there is a need for additional replication to discern clear patterns.

Fourth, very few studies have focused on the *mechanisms* leading voters to reward or punish corrupt behavior.[4] While a large body of literature has focused on country-level determinants of corruption, this study focuses on the role of the citizenry in changing or upholding electoral outcomes when candidates are accused of corruption. In contrast to work that has focused on economic voting – economic determinants that influence the voter's decision – this study is focused on *corruption voting*, which for the purposes of this analysis is defined as the study of voting behavior and public opinion in response to allegations of candidate corruption.[5] In examining factors like corruption, the work contributes to a literature on the role of informal institutions in shaping political outcomes (Guerriero, 2020; Helmke & Levitsky, 2004; Nannicini et al., 2013; North, 1990). A framework for Section 3 of this Element is dedicated to understanding the trade-offs voters make when faced with at least one corrupt candidate on the ballot. These trade-offs include the type of corruption the candidate engaged in, the state of the corruption allegation, legal action (including court decisions) taken in response to the allegation, and attributes of the candidate such as party, gender, race, and policy positions, among other

---

[4] Notable exceptions include Klašjna and Tucker (2013); Klašjna et al. (2016); Winters and Weitz–Shapiro (2013).

[5] I borrow the term "corruption voting" from Klašjna and Tucker (2013).

factors. Although the work advances the current literature on mechanisms, the research also comes with limitations. Some of the limitations include (1) survey respondents not being given incentives for their participation, (2) the outcome is a stated preference by the interviewee rather than an actual vote in a real election, and (3) as is the case with an intervention of this sort, the external validity of the results is always a question because the results are bounded in time, specific to the intervention utilized in the survey, and given in a particular spatial setting.

Finally, along with the refinement of positive theories, there also are important empirical and normative questions about the conditions under which certain types of corruption information will reduce turnout, and the extent to which information in elections should be designed to increase voter participation and electoral accountability. Having an empirical foundation for how the public perceives corruption can also serve as a helpful basis for creating interventions to change such norms and designing campaign finance reform and anti-corruption laws. This Element raises important implications for the potentially deleterious consequences of transparency efforts, and motivates an empirical and policy research agenda dedicated to understanding how laws that regulate libel, truthful information in campaigning, and free speech achieve desired outcomes for society. Similarly, the research raises issues about the participation and disclosure rules related to the activities of third parties such as interest groups in addition to candidate campaigns that could have an impact on participation and disclosure rules related to the activities of third parties and campaigns could also have an impact on the conditions under which voters reelect corrupt politicians.

To gain traction on these questions, it is important to establish conceptual clarity and a clear analytic framework. This Element proceeds by (1) defining the universe of corruption being discussed; (2) developing a conceptual framework for understanding the conditions under which voters punish or reward politicians accused of corruption; and (3) discussing mechanisms that would explain the conditions under which voters will punish or reward a politician with corruption allegations.

2 Electoral Accountability and Public Opinion

2.1 Corruption Definitions and Types

Prior to engaging in a discussion about different types of corruption, a working definition of corruption is in order. There is little doubt that corruption is a highly contested concept (Gallie, 1956). The goal here is not to argue for a particular definition of corruption, but rather to show important differences in how various actors have approached conceptualizing corruption. These definitions are then contrasted with popular conceptions of corruption. Defining candidate corruption is challenging, especially in the realm of public opinion, because it may not accord with definitions of the term offered by academics, courts, and statutes. Yet, the exercise is important because different types of corruption perceived by voters can determine whether politicians who commit allegedly corrupt acts will be reelected or not.

2.2 Formal Definitions of Corruption

One of the most popular conceptions of corruption in the academic literature, from Joseph Nye, involves "behavior which deviates from the formal duties of a public role because of private-regarding (personal, close family, clique) pecuniary or status gains; or violates the rules against the exercise of certain private-regarding influence" (Nye, 1967, p. 419). The emphasis on formal duties and rules (rather than norms) in this definition offers a more formalist approach to corruption, leading one to question the need, under certain conditions, for formal rules to be in place in order for the act to be defined as corrupt. A similar definition that has gained traction in academic, legal, and policy communities is Transparency International's definition: "the abuse of entrusted power for private gain." The term "private gain" can take many forms, but personal enrichment is certainly one of the most objectionable attributes that voters will find in the behavior of a politician, and most likely to punish. For corruption violations to be definitively punished by the electorate, they often have to be severe violations of social norms and the law, and often responded to by legal action (de Sousa & Moriconi, 2013). Where there is greater variation in voter responses is when conditions of illegality and personal enrichment are relaxed. For these reasons, some authors (e.g. Stephenson (2015)) choose to exclude legal campaign contributions, lobbying, and similar activities in their working definitions. While this may be appropriate because their work has different objectives, in evaluating the probability of voters punishing corrupt politicians, this aspect of corruption should be included in a definition of candidate corruption since it can both reflect and determine electoral behavior of voters.

2.3 Popular Conceptions

Political scientists and other social scientists have largely strayed away from conceptualizing corruption from the perspective of the public and from using the public interest as a criterion in a definition, mainly because the standards for corruption vary greatly across individuals, and it is difficult to define the public interest. The prominent anthropologist and political scientist James Scott states this difficulty clearly. "Corruption, we would all agree, involves a deviation from certain standards of behavior. The first question which arises is, What criteria shall we use to establish those standards?" (Scott, 1972).

Scott states that defining the public interest precisely and with agreement would be nearly impossible since that is an inherently ideological inquiry. Scott then discusses the difficulties of incorporating public opinion into a definition of corruption, and ultimately concludes that the diversity and ambiguity of views among the public as to what constitutes a corrupt act would make defining a corrupt act difficult. Scott concludes that the criteria one would use to determine a working definition would likely be arbitrary and problematic (Scott, 1972, 4).

The task of advancing any one conception of corruption that involves either defining public interest or discerning public opinion is resolutely difficult. That goal is distinct from categorizing those different views of corruption, and then using the definition to categorize the scope of inquiry for when voters punish "corrupt" politicians. One reason a discussion of how the public conceives of corruption is merited is because the majority of citizens hold a notion of corruption that is broader in scope than the way the term is used in academic literature or defined by the law.

To gain traction on these questions, it is important to first establish a clear analytic framework and to have conceptual clarity. This section proceeds by (1) discussing types of candidate corruption that factor into the decision by voters; and (2) developing a conceptual framework for understanding the conditions under which voters punish or reward politicians accused of corruption that includes key factors and hypotheses that determine when and why voters punish or support politicians accused of corruption.

2.4 Candidate Corruption Types in the Court of Public Opinion

To what extent do voters distinguish different types of corruption in candidates? What are the types of corruption that will lead voters to punish a politician in the voting booth? In this section, I argue that an important distinction is corruption that results in private enrichment versus corruption that is seen as "part of the political game." Electoral corruption can include a variety of actions as was seen in the introduction. Actions can include, but are not limited to bribery, vote buying, favoritism in procurement processes, nepotism, embezzlement, money laundering, and collusion (Botero et al., 2016). These different types of corruption not only have different consequences for society, but also are likely to result in different electoral outcomes, all else equal. The focus of this research is on elected officials, and not those involved in the civil service or private citizen actions (unless the individual decides to run for office, and a corruption allegation while the individual was a bureaucrat or private citizen factored into voting behavior). Corruption types viewed as enhancing one's personal wealth involve a benefit that only the politician receives, whereas clientelistic exchanges and campaign financing are more likely to be seen as having a broader benefit (Bardhan, 1997).

The electoral effects of different types of corruption types is under-explored in the literature. Truex (2011) examines the reaction of individuals to petty corruption (favoritism and small gifts) versus large-scale bribery in Nepal and finds toleration of petty corruption. The study contributes toward establishing a threshold of corruption that is acceptable in the minds of voters, but because the research design relies on observational data, the study cannot isolate the impact of corruption type on individual attitudes. In a more recent survey experiment in Argentina, Botero et al. (2016) randomized whether a candidate offered employment and construction materials; "misused public funds" and increased his personal wealth; or had no corruption. Their experimental design also allowed the authors to test the effect of partisanship and socioeconomic status on candidate evaluations. The authors found that voters punished corruption involving private enrichment more harshly. Surprisingly, they also found that wealthier respondents did not find one type of corruption less preferable to the other, whereas they differentiated between the two corruption types, selecting the clientelist candidate over the one who engaged in large-scale bribery (Botero et al., 2016). Their results contrasted with Weschle (2016), who found the opposite result in a survey experiment in India when manipulating how a politician spends funds he receives from a company for a political favor.

One critical dimension that has gone unstudied in previous studies are the trade-offs that voters make with respect to corruption type. The conjoint experiment in Section 3 not only experimentally manipulates corruption type and party, but also includes candidate policy positions, court decisions on political corruption, and attributes such as gender and affect. The design has the advantage of randomizing treatments, while offering a diverse set of choices when the voter has a ballot with at least one allegedly corrupt candidate.

2.5 Interpreting Voting Behavior Outcomes

The universe of voting behavior actions is both limited and relatively straightforward: (1) vote choice for a candidate, (2) casting a spoiled ballot or protest vote, or (3) abstention.[6] Yet, ascribing intention to those actions can prove challenging. This section elucidates voter intentions that stem from voting behavior when at least one politician on the ballot is accused of corruption.

Field interviews I have conducted in Brazil with political consultants and public opinion experts reveal a salient distinction made by Brazilian voters involving thresholds of "tolerable" corruption that lies between personal enrichment for taking public funds for private gain (contract kickbacks, bribery, etc.) versus impropriety related to buying public policy or illegally financing a campaign. In June 2005, Brazilian Congressional Deputy Roberto Jefferson, who at the time was under investigation for a corruption scandal with the Brazilian post office, claimed the *Partido dos Trabalhadores* (the Worker's Party, or PT) paid monthly "allowances" (*mensalão*) to congressmen of R$30,000 (approximately US$16,800) per month so that they would vote in line with President Luiz Inácio (Lula) da Silva. The scandal resulted in eight resignations and three removals of congressmen from office. Although empirical work by Rennó examining the effect of the *Mensalão* scandal concludes that the scandal did prevent candidates in the 2006 elections from seeking reelection and negatively affected the probability of reelection (Rennó, 2007), the importance of partisanship and performance on other issues such as the economy, ultimately had larger effects on voting behavior in the case of the president (Rennó, 2007).

The complexity of discerning the voter's motivation raises important concerns related to the measurement of voter motivation and implementing research designs that can rigorously identify the motivation of each voter type. Field experimental work which has examined the conditions under which voters punish or support corrupt politicians can only identify the effect that corruption information can have on a candidate's vote share, turnout, spoiled ballot, or protest vote behavior. Identification strategies that can show vote switching and underlying motivations are challenging to do and have yet to be done in the field. In this Element, I attempt to shed light on this behavior in a conjoint experiment in Section 4, where this issue is discussed in greater depth.

---

[6] Court decisions can shed light on the difficulty of regulating and deciphering the intention of write-in votes. In 1992, the US Supreme Court held in *Burdick* v. *Takushi* that Hawaii could enact a complete ban of write-in votes on the ballot. The case narrowed the holding of an earlier case, *Dixon* v. *Maryland State Administrative Board of Election Laws*, where the Fourth Circuit held that accommodating and counting write-in votes was legal for a fictional candidate, such as Donald Duck, since one's fundamental constitutional right included the right to say that no candidate was acceptable.

3 A Framework for Analyzing Candidate Corruption and Voting Behavior

Now that the scope of the concept for this Element has been defined, I turn to describing the conceptual framework for analyzing the conditions under which voters will reward or punish corrupt politicians. The framework presented in some of the most important individual- and macro-level factors that lead voters to punish, favor, or abstain from voting when at least one candidate is corrupt in an election.

The framework offers some new directions for research on the reelection of corrupt politicians. First, little of the existing literature has focused on the type of corruption that leads voters to punish politicians with corruption allegations. Second, the status of the corruption allegation offers a new dimension that the literature has overlooked. Third, the framework includes sources of corruption information that are broader than much of the extant literature, including informal and peer networks, which have yet to be included in much of the study of the reelection of allegedly corrupt politicians. Finally, the framework brings together individual- and macro-level factors that weigh into the voter's decision, which have largely been studied separately in previous literature.

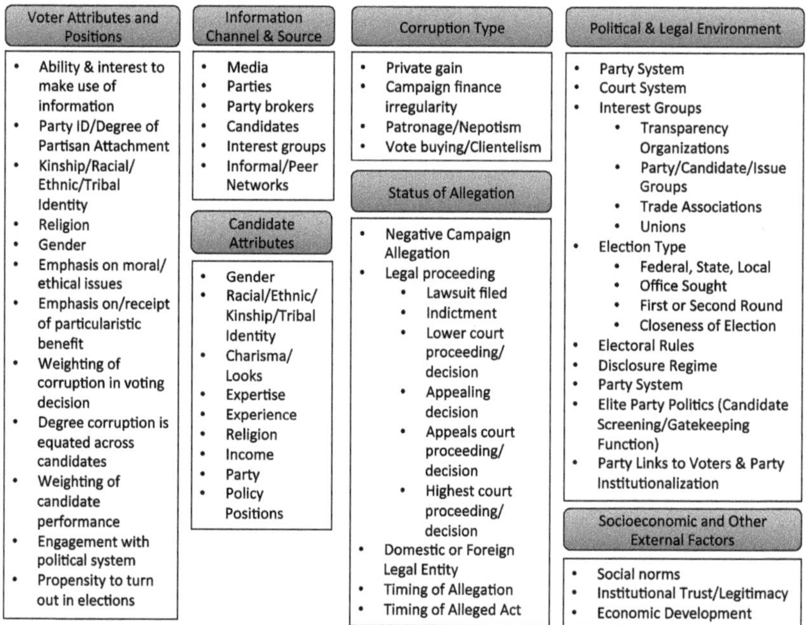

Figure 1 Factors influencing voter behavior toward a candidate with a corruption allegation

3.1 Information Channels and Sources of the Corruption Allegation

One important means of punishing corrupt politicians is to give voters information about the corrupt behavior, providing a potential basis to vote against such candidates. A theoretical literature focused on the effects of information on voting behavior concludes that under certain conditions, information improves accountability to mass publics (Alvarez, 1998; Besley & Burgess, 2002; Lupia & McCubbins, 1998; Przeworski et al., 1999). However, the empirical literature is still relatively scant on understanding the conditions under which information about corruption results in electoral accountability.

More generally, one hypothesis in the literature is that voters do not punish candidate corruption because they lack high-quality information to make a decision that would take corrupt politicians to task for their behavior (de Sousa & Moriconi, 2013; Ferraz & Finan, 2008; Humphreys & Weinstein, 2012). Reasons for this information deficit among citizens are numerous. In a number of developing countries, accountability structures such as a professionalized press corps, robust watchdog organizations, and transparency in government are not as commonplace. Access to information in certain developing countries may also be costly, especially for those in more rural areas, making the assessment of credible information more challenging.

Making valid causal inferences about these relationships is difficult, in large part because information about the corruption of politicians is rarely randomly assigned to voters. A number of studies with nonexperimental data that attempt to examine the effects of corruption charges on electoral performance find only modest effects (McCann & Dominguez, 1998; Peters & Welch, 1980). However, in a study of municipal governments in Brazil, Ferraz and Finan (2008) exploit randomized corruption audits, and find relatively large effects that ultimately decrease the probability of incumbent politicians being reelected; similarly a study by Chong et al. (2015) conducted in Mexico primarily shows a negative effect on incumbency. By contrast, in a randomized field experiment I conducted with F. Daniel Hidalgo and Yuri Kasahara, corruption information given to voters about the incumbent had no statistically significant effect on voting behavior, although both experimental studies reduced turnout. The turnout result thus places scope conditions on previous theories positing that more informed voters are more likely to turn out (Feddersen & Pesendorfer, 1996; Palfrey & Poole, 1987; Wolfinger & Rosenstone, 1980). Thus, while information about candidate corruption given to voters can enhance electoral accountability resulting in the punishment of corrupt politicians (Almeida, 2008; Anderson & Tverdova, 2003; Chang & Golden, 2004; Ferraz & Finan,

2008; Rennó, 2007; Winters & Weitz-Shapiro, 2013), there can be deleterious effects as well, including decreased voter turnout and reduced citizen confidence and trust in politicians and democratic institutions (Banerjee, Green, et al., 2010; Banerjee, Kumar, et al., 2010; Chong et al., 2015). Negative turnout effects can take place even in the presence of mandatory voting, and in some cases, voters are willing to bear the costs of absenteeism. Additionally, despite a number of papers that have shown that corruption is not a salient issue in the consciousness of many voters in the developing world (Almeida, 2008; Anderson & Tverdova, 2003; Chang & Golden, 2004; Rennó, 2007), experimental evidence has shown the opposite.

Field experimental work in this area is still nascent, and work that attempts to uncover the mechanisms that lead to these varied results is also relatively unexplored in the literature. The common feature of all the field experiments in this area is that they attempt to provide high quality and credible information that voters can easily digest. Work by Weitz-Shapiro and Winters (2017) and Botero et al. (2015) varies the corruption source in survey experiments in order to shed light on the effects of the credibility of individual sources. Specifically, Weitz-Shapiro and Winters (2014) vary whether corruption information in Brazil is disseminated via a federal corruption audit or from an opposing party, and the authors find that voters are more likely to punish the politician when the information comes from the audit. Botero et al. (2015) vary whether allegations coming from a reputable newspaper, the judiciary, or a well-respected nongovernmental organization (NGO) in Colombia. The authors find that the newspaper allegations have the strongest effect on voters punishing politicians with corruption allegations. This Element is an important first step toward understanding the role of the source of information as having an effect on corruption information.

Given the current electoral environment, there is a need to evaluate the efficacy of additional channels of information that are used to disseminate corruption information. The framework thus includes additional interest groups, parties and party brokers, and informal social networks as other actors that disseminate corruption information in important ways.

The survey experiment by Botero et al. (2015) and the field experiment conducted by de Figueiredo et al. (2023) present treatment conditions where corruption information is presented by an interest group. In the former case, respondents are given information by *Misión de Observación* (MOE), an election monitoring NGO, and in the latter case by the *Associação dos Magistrados Brasileiros* (AMB), a trade association of judges. Both of these NGOs, according to the respective authors, have a high degree of credibility with voters, and largely serve the purpose of disseminating truthful information in elections.

However, interest groups can also exist as extensions of intricate party networks, and can also be the originators of biased or even false information. In the United States, increased advertising expenditure on attack ads by interest groups is one of the most important and dramatic recent changes in elections (Brooks and Murov (2012)). Estimates of campaign ad spending during the 2016 US election cycle exceed $11 billion (Wesleyan Media Project (2016).[7] A prominent example, although not with corruption information, involved ads and a book promulgated by "Swift Boat Veterans for Truth," a 527 organization that questioned US presidential candidate John Kerry's service record during the Vietnam War. Although the group's accusations were later widely discredited, descriptive survey work has shown a possible negative impact on Kerry's vote share (Cheng & Riffe, 2008). The literature on negative campaigning reveals important mechanisms through which corruption information can have an impact on voting behavior. In discussing the efficacy of attack ads by "dark money" interest groups, Brooks and Murov (2012), p. 388 distinguish between two important concepts and mechanisms through which such information can shape voting behavior: effectiveness and persuasiveness.[8] They state that "effectiveness is not simply persuasion. Rather, net effectiveness in a two-candidate race is persuasion (movement of the target downward in terms of favorability) minus backlash (movement of the beneficiary of the negative ad downward in terms of favorability)," ultimately concluding that "[a]n ad is effective when it depresses support for the target more than it depresses support for the benefiting candidate" Brooks and Murov (2012), p. 388. Thus, both effectiveness and persuasion must be examined in order to determine the impact of corruption information on voting behavior. Doing so will take account of backlash, a reaction from voters that the negative message sent was unacceptable. Thus, understanding the conditions under which corruption information will be perceived as an "attack" versus truthful negative information will shape how the voter acts on the information, and one step that is needed is to see how information from a broader set of interest groups is received by the electorate. Moreover, survey experimental research should consider the possibility of measuring abstention as a possible response by individuals.

---

[7] In the wake of the passage of the Bipartisan Campaign Reform Act of 2002, and court decisions such as *Citizens United* v. *Federal Election Commission*, Super PACs, 527 organizations, and 501(c)(4) groups, abolished numerous restrictions on the establishment, funding, disclosure, and advertising for such interest groups. For additional context on these changes, see Fowler and Ridout (2010) and Brooks and Murov (2012).

[8] Brooks and Murov (2012) relate the mechanisms only to negative attack ads, but they can be applied to negative information more generally in elections.

In addition to interest groups, political parties not only convey information about candidates through a party label, but they also distribute information about candidates during elections. As such, in settings where clientelism is prominent, party and candidate "brokers" play an important role in the process. Although the party or candidate broker's role is important in voter mobilization (including vote or turnout buying) (e.g. Auyero (2001); Szwarcberg (2012)) and public goods provision (e.g. Levitsky (2003); Stokes et al. (2013); Gans–Morse et al. (2014)), their activities also include campaigning and disseminating information about candidates, including generating and responding to allegations of corruption. Zarazaga (2014, p. 30) succinctly states that "Scholars and the media have underestimated the most common way brokers have of winning votes: by campaigning. ...Given the price of airtime on national television and the low readership of newspapers in poor areas, mayors and their challengers rely mainly on local campaigns run by brokers." This role of the broker as a "propaganda activist" is enhanced by their simultaneous role as a reliable and trusted person in the community, where their enduring reputation for delivering on promises also enhances their credibility with information dissemination (Zarazaga, 2014, pp. 38–40).

3.2 Status of the Corruption Allegation

Another important factor largely overlooked in the literature is the status of the corruption allegation, which refers to the accuser or entity originating the accusation and any processes taken after the allegation is made or corruption action takes place. Status is distinguished from the allegation's source. The source relates to the information channel through which the voter receives news and updates of the candidate's alleged corruption. The status, by contrast, includes the initial accuser of the candidate's corruption or the process by which the corruption became known, and any related court, investigative, or other processes by which the details of the corruption are revealed. Thus, if an accusation is initially launched by a newspaper or interest group about a candidate's corruption, the newspaper or interest group would be part of the allegation's status and also a source for voters to access information about the candidate's corruption. If the accuser is an individual citizen who witnessed or took part in a corrupt act, he/she would not be considered the information channel for that act; rather, for the purposes of this study, the accuser would be considered part of the allegation's status and not part of the source or information channel for the voter.

Examining the process by which an alleged act of corruption is generated and then goes through the legal system, government investigation, or other process, reveals moments that can be predictive of a candidate's support or demise. One additional feature worth noting is that the evidentiary burden can be relatively low, especially in the early stages of an arrest or the court process. Yet, the action of an arrest or an indictment can lead voters to "convict" in the "court of public opinion." Noticing the distance between the evidentiary burden required in a corruption allegation process, and how predictive it is not only of the person's ultimate guilt, but their demise in future elections sheds light on the power that actors such as prosecutors and judges have in shaping public opinion, and the trust that voters have in the justice system. The mere threat of a lawsuit or investigation involving political corruption may reduce a candidate's prospects for reelection. Despite these possibilities, rigorous work on the effects of public opinion in response to corruption prosecutions, investigations, and court decisions is still in its infancy.

The extent to which voters have trust in prosecutors and judges will likely determine their likelihood of punishing politicians accused of corruption. If voters trust prosecutors and the judiciary and understand the nature of justice system procedures and rulings, then court decisions on corruption – whether they are convictions or not – are likely to serve as credible information informing voters of corruption. If there is distrust in prosecutors and the judiciary, then two outcomes are most likely: (1) all else equal, voters who perceive the court to be committing more Type II errors (failing to convict the guilty) than Type I errors (convicting the innocent) and will only be responsive to judicial decisions when a conviction is handed down; or (2) *ceteris paribus*, the court decision will have no effect on the voter's decision. The introduction of appeals adds complexity to the situation.[9] In Section 4 of this Element, one treatment condition varies court rulings on candidate corruption, and examines the effects on voting for candidates in a conjoint survey experiment conducted in Brazil. To the best of my knowledge, this is the first experimental intervention to examine the effect of public corruption court rulings on voting behavior.

3.3 Candidate Attributes

Voters not only look at a candidate's corruption, but they also weigh their decision in light of the candidate's policy positions, performance, and attributes. An established literature in American politics examines the effect of candidates'

---

[9] The extant literature on prosecution of corruption is still emerging. Gordon (2009) develops a formal model and uses a regression discontinuity design to test for partisan bias in corruption prosecutions, and finds partisan bias in federal corruption prosecutions in the Clinton and Bush (II) Justice Departments, although the results may understate the bias for Bush (II) while overstating the bias for Clinton. He found the crackdown increased citizen trust of the regime. In a review article, Gordon and Huber (2009) suggest the need for further research in this area.

traits on voting behavior (e.g. Bartels, 2002; Campbell et al., 1960; Funk, 1996; Hayes, 2005). Although early works such as Campbell et al. (1960) emphasized the importance of candidate traits, the focus on candidate attributes became subordinated to the role of party identification, issue ownership, and other "rational" determinants of voting (Funk, 1996, pp. 1–2). A body of survey research in the 1980s and 1990s established a strong link between candidate traits and voter attitudes (Markus, 1982; Kinder, 1986). Traits have included the candidate's intelligence, competence, empathy, warmth, and trustworthiness, among others.

Traits and "trait ownership" (Hayes, 2005) can play an important role in the voter's decision when corruption allegations surface in an election. In a survey experiment manipulating candidates' competence and warmth in response to marital infidelity or tax evasion, Funk (1996) found that both competence and warmth improved candidate evaluations, but competence had a greater effect. Other attributes include the extent to which the voter identifies with the candidate (Warner and Banwart, 2016), which can heighten the probability of forgiveness for a corrupt act. In Section 4, I offer, to the best of my knowledge, the first experimental evidence of candidate evaluations that includes these traits in order to see how they factor into candidate evaluations, when policy preferences, corruption type, and party are also included as treatment conditions, but are conceptually included as control variables.

3.3.1 Gender, Race, and Other "Fixed" Characteristics

The candidate's traits are also shaped by visible features such as gender and race, which may have an impact on voter's support of a clean or corrupt politician. A literature exploring the effect of gender and corruption voting has only recently emerged. The majority of the literature examines the effect of women in politics on perceptions and actual levels of corruption (e.g. Dollar & Fismangatti, 2001; Swamy et al., 2001).[10] According to Esarey and Chirillo (2013, p. 365), the assumption that women are more harshly punished for corruption has only been "anecdotally observed in American politics." Outside the United States, Jackson and Smith (1996) present a case study of punishment of female politicians for corruption in Australia, and Mancuso et al. (1998) demonstrate from interviews that the belief is present in Canada. In Section 4, the conjoint experiment has gender as a treatment condition, which will shed light on whether female politicians are punished more harshly than their male counterpoints for corruption. To the best of my knowledge, little, if any, work has

---

[10] For an in-depth review of this literature, see Esarey and Chirillo (2013).

been done that explicitly looks at the impact of race, age, and other candidate characteristics on the impact of corruption.

3.3.2 Political Party

Few studies have examined how voters and politicians react to corruption scandals, and the study of partisans is particularly important because providing information to strong partisans might be a useful strategy that corrupt politicians rely on to secure support. A relatively consistent and unsurprising finding in the literature is that strong partisans are the least likely to punish politicians with allegations of corruption (Anduiza et al., 2013; Slomczynski & Shabad, 2012; Winters & Weitz–Shapiro, 2015). Thus, in more highly institutionalized party systems, where links to bases of support are stronger and where a higher barrier for candidate entry is imposed, the probability of a corrupt politician appearing on the ballot decreases. In such systems, the meaning of a party label and party socialization carries greater weight, possibly serving as a signal for voters to sort between corrupt and clean politicians (de Sousa & Moriconi, 2013).

Although the lower barriers to entry, and party brand recognition in weakly institutionalized party systems are less likely to prohibit the entry and punishment of corrupt candidates, high party competition (which can take place in highly and weakly institutionalized party systems) can increase the chances of credible information about corrupt politicians being disseminated. This increased accountability can result in electoral punishment, if voters are responsive to corruption information (de Sousa & Moriconi, 2013; Mainwaring & Torcal, 2006).

Finally, the presence of an anti-corruption party, as discussed elsewhere in this section and the next section, can have important effects in raising the salience of the issue in elections. It also can lead to defection when a candidate with corruption allegations appears on the ballot from that party, as is the case in the experiments presented in the next section.

3.4 Voter Attributes and Positions

What attributes of voters lead them to be more likely to punish corrupt politicians? A number of studies in the literature focus on voters' inability to monitor the behavior of politicians or exercise their right to vote either because of institutional constraints or because of obfuscatory actions of the politician (e.g. Chang & Golden, 2007; Myerson, 1993; Persson et al., 2003), while assuming a homogeneous electorate (Klašjna et al., 2016). In this section, I focus on the attributes that are most prevalent in the voting behavior and corruption literature, or that have emerged from the research I have conducted.

3.4.1 Partisan Attachment

Partisanship – characterized by a psychological attachment to a particular political party – often has an important influence on citizen perceptions of democratic institutions, candidates, and voting behavior. While studies of party identification in terms of mass politics have a rich line of inquiry in the American and European politics literature (Achen, 2002; Bartolini & Mair, 1990; Campbell et al., 1960; Green et al., 2002; Miller & Shanks, 1996), its dynamics are quite different and relatively under-studied in new democracies, in part because the role of parental socialization during recent democratic transitions is oftentimes much less pronounced (Achen, 2002; Converse, 1969; Jennings & Niemi, 1981). Although the socialization process might be different, there is evidence of stable partisan identification and preferences in some newer democracies (see, e.g. (Samuels, 2006) for Brazil and (McCann & Lawson, 2003) for Mexico). At the same time, however, a number of forces work against this trend in these countries. Intergenerational partisan attachments are often not present when a host of new parties emerged after a recent democratic transition. Moreover, Mainwaring and Torcal (2006) rightly point out that most democracies in developing countries also have higher electoral volatility, weaker ideological and programmatic links with voters, and stronger direct links between candidates and voters. Thus, voters in settings with weak party institutionalization are likely to respond to corruption allegations differently than in advanced industrialized countries. All else equal, overall levels of partisanship will be lower, party ties are less likely to induce loyalty in the face of corruption allegations, and candidate switching and spoiled ballots cast either as "voice" or "exit" will be higher (Gingerich, 2009; Klašjna & Tucker, 2013; Winters & Weitz–Shapiro, 2015).

One other important mechanism at work discussed in the next section and also mentioned by Klašjna et al. (2016) is the salience of corruption brought about by the presence of an anti-corruption party in the electoral arena. Specifically, the authors point to how an anti-corruption party raises the salience of corruption in society, leading large segments of society to engage in *sociotropic corruption voting*, or "vote choice influenced by [the] perception of corruption in society" (Klašjna et al., 2016, p. 70). While this is "one side of the coin," field and survey experimental work discussed in the next section, coupled with a conjoint experiment that follows point to a backlash that can take place when voters feel betrayed by an anti-corruption party. Specifically, unlike voters who may respond with denial or by increasing their threshold for corruption when faced with a trade-off between party loyalty and voting for a corrupt candidate (Anduiza et al., 2013), when provided information about corruption, voters from an anti-corruption party are more likely to be intensely negative than nonpartisans or voters from other parties. For this reason, the weighting of corruption in the voting decision is a factor included in the framework given in Figure 1.

3.4.2 Education, Political Awareness, and Engagement

Since much of the population in the field experiment conducted by de Figueiredo et al. (2023) had relatively low education, their changed behavior is likely to be consistent with theories that suggest that information about candidate behavior will lead less informed voters to update their assessments of politicians (Arceneaux, 2007; Malhotra & Kuo, 2008) and also involves assessments of candidate performance (retrospective voting) (Key, 1966; Fiorina, 1981; Winters & Weitz–Shapiro, 2013). These contrast with theories emphasizing partisan cues as important heuristics that permit less informed voters to act as if they are informed (e.g. Bullock, 2011; Jackman & Sniderman, 2002; Lupia & McCubbins, 1998), and a body of work that emphasizes a lack of updating of priors so that the voter's views are stable and consistent with existing political beliefs (e.g. Zaller, 1992). Yet, it is important to realize that those theories likely do hold for those who remain loyal to other parties.[11]

Another important body of literature that was mentioned in an earlier section posits that highly informed and more educated voters are more likely to punish corrupt politicians (de Sousa & Moriconi, 2013; Klašjna et al., 2016; Winters & Weitz–Shapiro, 2015). Reasons for this dynamic include the motivation and ability of these voters to better distinguish different types of corruption, see the harmful impact of corruption in their life and community, and differentiate evidentiary burdens for corruption accusations. Finally, the possibility exists that poorer voters, although more likely to receive particularistic benefits in clientelistic settings, are less ideological than more highly educated voters, which can increase the chance of partisan attachment resulting in the support of a corrupt politician (Klašjna et al., 2016). However, de Sousa and Moriconi (2013) point out that this proposition is still highly contested. One thing to keep in mind is that the theories discussed at the beginning of this section may apply to certain types of voters (like those who rank corruption highly), while theories emphasizing awareness and education could apply to other types of voters.

---

[11] In the conjoint experiment that follows, we did not feel we had reliable enough education information on respondents to include it in the study.

3.5 Political and Legal Environment

One could imagine citizens responding in a variety of ways to court decisions involving corruption. If voters trust the judiciary and understand the nature of its rulings, then court decisions on corruption – whether they are convictions or not – are likely to serve as credible information informing voters of corruption. Assuming that corruption figures prominently in their voting decision, these voters will likely follow the court's lead on whether or not there is a conviction.

If there is distrust in the judiciary, then two outcomes are most likely in the case of electoral candidate corruption: (1) all else equal, voters will perceive the court to be committing more Type II errors (failing to convict the guilty) than Type I errors (convicting the innocent) and will be more responsive to convictions, since not guilty verdicts are more likely to be the result of error and signals of conviction are more likely to be informative; or (2) *ceteris paribus*, the court decision will have no effect on the voter's decision since there is a disregard for the court's legitimacy.

3.6 Socioeconomic and Other External Factors

To date, very little work has been done on the extent to which voters hold politicians accountable for corruption in different socioeconomic conditions. The lack of literature is understandable; approaching this question in a causal manner presents challenges since economic conditions can be correlated with many other factors. In comparing the reaction of voters to economic conditions in Sweden (a low corruption country) and Moldova (a high corruption country), Klašjna and Tucker (2013) find that Swedish voters punish corrupt politicians equally, irrespective of the economy. Moldovan voters, by contrast, are more likely to punish allegedly corrupt politicians when the economic conditions are more challenging. The economy is a proxy for performance of the politician, and perhaps not surprisingly, voters in more challenging economic conditions are more likely to assign blame to incumbents for an economic downturn. Moreover, the corrupt act – especially involving private enrichment – can accentuate inequality and create greater resentment when an elite politician enriches himself while citizens are suffering during difficult economic times. When economic times are good, voters are more likely to be attracted to the politician's competence and even believe that the officeholder should stay in power for the prosperous economy to continue (de Sousa & Moriconi, 2013).

In addition to the economy, electoral rules can also shape the extent to which voters will punish corrupt politicians. First, the number of candidates in the election can influence the extent to which voters will make an informed voting decision. In a novel survey experiment in Brazil, Aguilar et al. (2015) examined the impact of the candidate's race on vote choice. The authors found that with only a few candidates on the ballot, respondents selected candidates without regard to race. As the ballot size increased with more candidate choices, white and non-white respondents were more likely to choose a candidate of their own race. With corrupt candidates, the role of information provision and the salience of corruption as an issue is likely to be more important in settings where there are more candidates on the ballot. Thus, all else equal, corrupt candidates are more likely to be punished in second round elections, where voters can scrutinize each candidate in greater detail, increasing the probability that the allegedly corrupt act will be known to voters. In addition, whether electoral punishment is more likely in local and regional elections than in national elections is unclear and likely to be context-specific. In localities where clientelism is prominent, voters may be able to punish political machines that do not deliver on promises, but on the other hand, the monitoring of votes may diminish the chance that a corrupt political machine would be voted out of power. Whether or not clientelism is present, voters are likely to have greater ease in seeing the provision of public services and if corruption is undermining efficiency and quality of services. However, as de Sousa and Moriconi (2013, p. 482) point out, in most countries, mayors spend but do not tax and voters are more likely to be hostile to those levying taxes.

The screening of candidates, either by parties or electoral entry rules, can also prevent potential candidates involved in corruption from entering the political arena. Scholars have pointed out that the higher entry barriers of single- or multi-member districts relative to proportional representation systems, the absence of party list voting, and high party competition all increase electoral accountability and reduce the likelihood of corrupt candidates having a place on the ballot (de Sousa et al., 2013; Kurer, 2005; Kunicova & Rose-Ackerman, 2005; Myerson, 1993; Persson et al., 2003).[12]

Taken together, this section offers an in-depth look at when and why voters punish corrupt politicians. The framework includes interplay of macro- and micro-levels that work to determine whether voters will punish or support allegedly corrupt politicians. The complex interplay of political, economic, and social forces suggests that variation in voter response to corruption should not be viewed solely as a valence issue as a number of scholars have done in the past (Ansolabehere & Snyder, 2000; Clark, 2009; Curini, 2015; Curini & Martelli, 2010; Green, 2007; Stokes, 1963).

---

[12] In the conjoint experiment we do later in this Element, these are operationalized as control variables in the core specifications.

4 Corruption and the Voter's Decision: Evidence from a Conjoint Experiment

Why do voters keep reelecting corrupt politicians? How do voters select among a variety of positive, negative, and neutral characteristics of candidates, especially when faced with candidates accused of corruption? For example, to what extent do party allegiances and policy alignment mitigate a candidate's corruption? When do voters "convict" a candidate in the court of public opinion if the candidate has been found guilty of corruption by a judge in a court? What levels of candidate corruption are tolerated and punished by voters?

Drawing from the conceptual framework presented in the previous section, these research questions are studied in this section utilizing a conjoint experiment, which allows for an understanding of the micro-foundations that underpin corruption voting.[13] Specifically, the experiment manipulates different types of corruption and signals of the corruption by manipulating the behavior of court, prosecutor, and criminal defense lawyer decisions on corruption. In addition, the conjoint experiment also manipulates a variety of candidate attributes including candidate parties, policy positions, and biographical attributes such as gender and experience, in order to analyze the causal effect of each characteristic on an individual's vote choice. While these variables are only a subset of the factors mentioned in the framework discussed in the previous section, statistical power and other on-the-ground concerns prevented the entire framework from being tested.[14] The conjoint experiment allows for the causal identification of trade-offs that voters make when faced with one or more corrupt candidates.

Understanding how voters make decisions when faced with a corrupt candidate is a complex process. Voters are forced to prioritize and aggregate their preferences along numerous dimensions,[15] including candidate attributes and policy positions, and ultimately choose a candidate or decide not to vote.[16] When faced with a candidate accused of corruption, that choice often involves

---

[13] Corruption voting is defined here as the effect of candidate corruption on voting behavior. Klašnja, Lupu, and Tucker (2021, p. 2) define the term corruption voting slightly more broadly as "the effect of corruption on voting behavior, analogous to the term economic voting."

[14] The items included in the conjoint experiment were selected based on context-specific factors based on field interviews with a variety of actors in the political system and based on the existing literature.

[15] The literature on preference aggregation in elections is well-established, dating back to the seminal work of Downs (1957) who drew on Hotelling (1929)'s spatial model of firm competition and Black (1958)'s median voter theorem (Dewan & Shepsle, 2011). For reviews of this literature, see Dewan and Shepsle (2011); Powell (2007).

[16] In systems with compulsory voting, there is also a decision as to whether to cast a spoiled ballot.

making trade-offs along other dimensions. Those trade-offs have significant implications for electoral accountability and for understanding how voters make multidimensional choices.

The conjoint experiment is conducted through a nationally representative survey in Brazil, a country that has been rocked by political corruption in recent years. To name a few examples, corruption scandals have led to the imprisonment of former president Luiz Inácio Lula da Silva, the impeachment of former president Dilma Rousseff, and criminal proceedings against former president Michel Temer. Although these national corruption scandals play an important role in shaping Brazil's political and economic trajectory, the country has subnational variation in corruption levels, income inequality, and partisan attachment, while also maintaining strong prosecutorial and judicial institutions to combat corruption. A number of aspects of Brazil's institutions and voting behavior generalize to other settings. First, as Domingo (2004); Ferejohn (2002); Pavão (2019); Sieder, Schjolden, and Angell (2005); Stone Sweet (2000), and others have pointed out, a global trend in both the developed and developing world has emerged where courts are engaging in policy making, limiting the power of legislatures and regulating the conduct of politicians. The phenomenon, termed the "judicialization of politics" also involves courts deciding on whether politicians are guilty of corruption. Not only do their decisions have direct effects on politicians, but they also have effects on public opinion, especially since courts can establish norms for what is acceptable in the political arena (Pavão, 2019). Second, both corruption levels and types are varied and take place on a large scale in Brazil,[17] making it possible to study numerous trade-offs made with a wide range of possible types of malfeasance. At the same time, anti-corruption forces – including corruption auditing, prosecutorial efforts, and judicial independence – are also sophisticated, providing the opportunity to examine their efficacy in shaping public opinion.

This study's central contributions are both substantive and methodological. First, the conjoint experiment enables the possibility of isolating and testing rigorously the causal effect of corruption types on voting behavior. Doing so allows one to determine when voters will punish corrupt politicians and observe thresholds of toleration for different types of illicit behavior by politicians. Prior work trying to explain when and why voters punish or support corrupt politicians fails to address fully the complexity of this

---

[17] For example, Power and Taylor (2011, p. 7) state that corruption is "readily apparent" in interest articulation and aggregation; policymaking; and policy implementation and adjudication in Brazil.

decision process. Studies solely relying on observational data are subject to endogeneity since vote choice may influence one's perception of corruption, instead of the other way around, as a number of studies have mentioned (e.g. Anderson & Tverdova, 2003; Anduiza et al., 2013; Klašjna & Tucker, 2013). Field experimental work informing voters of candidate corruption and looking at the effects on voting behavior (e.g. Banerjee, Green, Green, & Pande, 2010; Banerjee, Kumar, Pande, & Su, 2011; Chong et al., 2015; de Figueiredo et al., 2023; Humphreys & Weinstein, 2012), is effective in addressing the causal effect of the information on voting behavior, but typically fails to rigorously test mechanisms that lead the voters to punish or support corrupt politicians. Survey experiments attempting to address mechanisms are often limited by the number of treatment conditions that can be implemented because of statistical power constraints (e.g. Botero et al., 2015; Botero et al., 2021; Winters & Weitz–Shapiro, 2013, 2015). Second, the design also allows the legitimacy of institutions such as courts to be measured through an actual voting decision, rather than by soliciting perceptions directly from respondents. Measuring legitimacy by asking respondents their perceptions of institutions can be problematic because legitimacy itself is a complex concept that is "too unwieldy and complex to measure with one indicator" (McCullough, 2015, p. 2). In addition, expressing dissatisfaction to an authority figure may not be the optimal response for interviewees, increasing the possibility of social desirability bias in survey responses. Finally, as has been documented in the psychology literature, respondents often do not have an accurate sense of their own behavior.

4.1 Candidate Corruption and the Voter's Multidimensional Decision

Do different types of corruption by politicians lead voters to change their chances of voting for a candidate? A number of scholars have posited important distinctions between corruption, including "grand" versus "petty" corruption, and corruption of high level political officials versus bureaucrats versus private individuals (Botero et al., 2021). The focus of this research is predominantly on elected officials, unless an individual decides to run for office, and had a corruption allegation while the individual was a bureaucrat or private citizen that factored into the candidate's voting behavior. Previous literature that has examined the impact of corruption type on voter attitudes has shown that the impact of scandals unrelated to the candidate's office and undermining the individual's moral standing had a larger impact on voters than corruption involving abuses of power in office (Funk, 1996; Welch & Hibbing, 1997). The work of Truex

(2011) and Botero et al. (2021), discussed earlier in this Element shed light on these dynamics.

Like the Botero et al. (2021) study, this study randomizes corruption types, ensuring that unobserved factors correlated with the type of corruption are not confounding results. This study also examines effects relative to other voter preferences, which give a greater sense of the trade-offs voters are making, and also likely results in magnitudes that map more closely to actual voting behavior.

Finally, there has been very recent work that utilizes conjoint analysis to study corruption voting. Most notably, Klašnja et al. (2021) examine the effects of corruption voting in Argentina, Chile, and Uruguay, manipulating (1) whether a candidate is accused of taking bribes or is praised for anti-corruption efforts, (2) the information source of the corruption, (3) economic performance of the candidate, (4) party affiliation, and (5) gender. In contrast to the results of this study, they find much larger treatment effects of the corruption treatment which ranges from a 27 to 36 percentage point reduction in the likelihood of the candidate receiving a vote.

Court Decisions. One important contrast with previous electoral field experiments, including work by de Figueiredo et al. (2023), was the difference in court decisions that candidates had experienced going into the election. In the São Paulo study that informed voters about the corruption convictions of politicians, mayoral candidate Gilberto Kassab had a conviction that was later overturned, while candidate Marta Suplicy had a conviction that was being appealed at the time of the election. Moreover, a number of national legislators in Brazil either have been convicted of corruption and other crimes, or have cases pending against them. Yet, to date, little work has examined the effect of court decisions on corruption on voting behavior.

One could imagine citizens responding in a variety of ways to court decisions involving corruption. If voters trust the judiciary and understand the nature of its rulings, then court decisions on corruption, whether they are convictions or not, are likely to be seen as credible information educating voters of corruption. If there is distrust in the judiciary, then two outcomes are most likely: (1) all else equal, voters who perceive the court to be committing more Type II errors (failing to convict the guilty) than Type I errors (convicting the innocent) will only be responsive to judicial decisions when a conviction is handed down; or (2) *ceteris paribus*, the court decision will have no effect on the voter's decision. In addition, if the probability of voting for a candidate decreases based on a case being filed by a prosecutor – even if the defendant is found to be not guilty – possible conclusions to be drawn include a high respect for prosecutors, or a high disenchantment with politicians and/or the judiciary.

Policy Positions. To what extent do voters factor in policy positions of candidates in their voting decision? Understanding the extent to which individual policies factor into vote choice allows us to examine the extent to which the preferences of individuals within a given area align with their representative's voting decisions and policies. Voters may knowingly vote for a corrupt politician, because of their alignment with the candidate's policy preferences and expected delivery on policies that are of benefit to the voter (Pande, 2011; Winters & Weitz–Shapiro, 2013). Winters and Weitz–Shapiro (2013) term this dynamic the "tradeoff hypothesis," and evidence from the literature includes Rundquist, Strom, and Peters (1977) (finding in lab experiments that voters are less likely to punish candidates whose policies align with their own preferences), Peters and Welch (1980) (finding variation in punishment of candidates for the US House of Representatives), and Banerjee et al. (2010) (finding that voters in northern India punished based on the candidate's ethnicity and performance).

Party. In new democracies, the role of parental socialization during recent democratic transitions is oftentimes much less pronounced than in settings with more entrenched political parties (Achen, 2002; Converse, 1969; Jennings & Niemi, 1981). Although the socialization process might be different, there is evidence of stable partisan identification and preferences in some newer democracies (see, e.g. Samuels (2006) for Brazil and McCann and Lawson (2003) for Mexico). Barros, Goldszmidt, and Pereira (2019), in a survey experiment in Brazil, also found that voters are more likely to elect a corrupt candidate when the candidate is of their own party.

At the same time, however, a number of forces work against this trend. Intergenerational partisan attachments are often not present when a host of new parties have emerged after a recent democratic transition. Moreover, Mainwaring and Torcal (2006) rightly point out that most democracies in developing countries also have high electoral volatility, weak ideological and programmatic links with voters, and strong direct links between candidates and voters. Thus, voters in settings with weak party institutionalization are likely to respond to corruption allegations differently than those in advanced industrialized countries. All else equal, overall levels of partisanship will be lower, party ties are less likely to induce loyalty in the face of corruption allegations, and candidate switching and spoiled ballots cast either as "voice" or "exit" will be higher (Gingerich, 2009; Klašjna & Tucker, 2013; Winters & Weitz–Shapiro, 2015).

One other important mechanism at work that emerged from the field experiment conducted by de Figueiredo et al. (2023), and also mentioned by Klašjna et al. (2016), is the salience of corruption brought about by the presence of an anti-corruption party in the electoral arena. Specifically, the authors point to how an anti-corruption party raises the salience of corruption in society, leading large segments of society to engage in *sociotropic corruption voting*, or "vote choice influenced by [the] perception of corruption in society" (Klašjna et al., 2016, p. 70). Although the Worker's Party (PT) arguably had a reputation as an anti-corruption party in the years before the field experiment took place, by the time this conjoint experiment was completed, that was completely gone in the wake of the *Mensalão* and *Lava Jato* corruption scandals. In addition, legislators were seriously considering launching impeachment proceedings against President Rousseff.

Gender. One possible reason why female politicians are underrepresented in positions of political power could be that voters discriminate against them. The sources of this discrimination can come from voters, who may believe women are ill-suited for politics, or are inferior. They also could stem from more subtle biases involving gender discrimination that the voter is not yet aware of.[18]

Two recent conjoint experiments cut against the discrimination hypothesis. Work by Broockman, Carnes, Crowder–Meyer, and Skovron (2021) suggested that female politicians not only did not encounter overt discrimination from respondents, they even received a favorable rating from voters relative to similarly situated male politicians. Teele et al. (2018) find strong positive increases in the probability that one would vote for a female candidate relative to a similarly situated male. They argue that party gatekeepers are discriminating against women, which ultimately limits the candidate pool.

Gender has become an important issue in Brazilian politics. On August 31, 2016, the Senate impeached President Dilma Rousseff, Brazil's first female president, by a vote of 61–20 for relying on *pedaladas fiscais* – for using public bank funds to finance social programs – a violation of budgetary laws. The motivations for the impeachment are complex, but sexism was raised as a factor in her impeachment. Groups such as *Mulheres Pela Democracia* (Women for Democracy) were created to support Rousseff. The press and feminist groups mentioned that male politicians who had committed similar acts or even engaged in corruption for personal enrichment were not prosecuted, and protesters in the streets cited gender bias in the impeachment (Achen, 2016; Fávero, 2016), so it is credible that female politicians are punished more harshly for corruption allegations.

Scholars have long noted the importance of attributes in the voting decision (Cain et al., 1987; Pitkin, 1967). Yet, to date, few have been able to isolate

---

[18] For a more extensive review of the gender discrimination literature, see Teele, Kalla, and Rosenbluth (2018).

rigorously the effect of attributes on voting behavior and also quantify their effects relative to other factors in the voting decision. The challenge of investigating attributes is that they are highly correlated with many other observed and unobserved factors. The random assignment of attributes to candidates in the conjoint design results in a more rigorous approach where the impact of the attribute is isolated. The selection process for attributes is discussed in greater detail in the section that follows.

4.2 Experimental and Survey Design

The survey was part of Ipsos's national omnibus survey in Brazil, which included a probability sample of 1,200 face-to-face interviews in 72 municipalities throughout the country. The sample is representative of urban areas in Brazil, and has a margin of error of 3 percentage points. Additional details of the sample of the survey are available in Appendixes A and B. The research team conducted training sessions with interviewers, and piloted the survey prior to the launch of the omnibus survey in the field. Based on the piloting of the survey, I have good reason to believe respondents understood the exercise and took it seriously.

One advantage of the conjoint design is that it does not directly ask about candidate corruption, policy positions, and personal attributes. In addition, the enumerators and respondents are not told about gender, corruption, and policy positions of the candidates out of concern for social desirability bias among respondents.

Figure 2 shows a sample conjoint table from the experiment. Names were chosen from the most common first and last names in Brazil that clearly identified the gender of the candidate. I selected "generic" last names that were not tied to dynastic political families. I also chose not to explicitly have gender as an attribute, both to increase external validity (by simulating a real ballot) and to reduce the chances of social desirability bias.

Table 1 shows the universe of attributes and levels used in the conjoint experiment. The first attribute, corruption type, offers the candidate not facing any corruption allegations. This level was one of the few cases where the level had to be "linked" to a level for another attribute; if the candidate did not have corruption allegations, he/she could not be subject to court proceedings.[19] Both in the pilot and in field interviews with survey experts and political consultants, I found that voters widely understood the wording of the level for the

---

[19] Since Portuguese has gendered nouns and adjectives, I also had to link candidates with the proper gendered wording, but I have no reason to believe this linking would have an effect on outcomes.

Perfil

Candidato	Luiz Santos	Camila Barbosa
Cargo	Ex-vereador	Ex-vereador
Partido	PMDB	PT
Acusações de corrupção	Não foi acusado de nada.	Foi acusada por aceitar um suborno para um contrato de uma obra.
Situação dos processos judiciais	Não foi acusado de nada.	Foi condenada em primeira instância e está recorrendo da decisão.
Maioridade Penal	A favor da redução da maioridade penal.	A favor da redução da maioridade penal.
Posição do candidato frente ao aborto	Contra a legalização do aborto.	A favor da legalização do aborto.
Posição a respeito do gasto público (ajuste fiscal do governo)	Melhorar a saúde, a educação e asistência social mesmo que deva aumentaro o gasto público.	Melhorar a saúde, a educação e asistência social mesmo que deva aumentaro o gasto público.
Principal característica do candidato	Com grande capacidade intelectual e profissional.	Próximo do povo/conhece seus problemas.

Figure 2 Sample conjoint table given to respondents (in Portuguese)

kickback to be a form of corruption that resulted in private enrichment. I chose the three selected policy issues based on their salience in newspapers, accessibility to voters, and high ranking in opinion polls as important issues at the time.

Brazil's party system is highly fragmented, and so party labels do not convey high informational content in the way they do in countries with more highly institutionalized party systems. In the 2016 elections, there were thirty-five registered parties, and twelve more parties awaited registration from the *Tribunal Superior Eleitoral* (TSE, or Superior Electoral Tribunal). This point is discussed in greater detail in the next section, but because of the highly fragmented nature of the party system, I felt justified in doing a full randomization of parties and policy positions. The four parties chosen – DEM, PMDB, PSDB, and PT – are large parties that represent a broad ideological

Table 1 Candidate attributes and levels

Attributes	Levels
Corruption type	[No corruption allegations]
	Accused of accepting an illegal campaign contribution
	Accused of accepting a kickback for a government work contract
Court proceedings	[No court proceedings]
	Found guilty by a trial court
	Found not guilty by a trial court
	Found guilty by a trial court and currently appealing the decision
	Found not guilty in the trial court, and the prosecution is appealing the decision
	Found not guilty in the trial court, and guilty on appeal
	Found guilty in the trial court, and not guilty on appeal
Abortion	[Against legalizing abortion]
	In favor of legalizing abortion
Criminal age of majority	[Against reducing the criminal age of majority]
	In favor of reducing the criminal age of majority
Public spending	[Reduce public spending, even if it would reduce funding for health, education and social assistance]
	Improve health, education and social assistance even if public spending increases
Party	DEM
	PMDB
	PSDB
	[PT]
Names (gender)	*Male Names:* Matheus Oliveira, Luiz Santos, João Silva, Pedro Souza
	Female Names: Julia Almeida, Camila Barbosa, Vitória Lima, Luiza Rodrigues
Principal characteristic	[Experience in public administration]
	High intellectual and professional capacity
	Proven leadership ability
	Close to the people/knows their problems

Note: Baseline levels are in brackets. Due to power and logistical constraints, the entire universe of permutations of court rulings such as being found guilty in the trial court and guilty on appeal are not included in the conjoint design. Despite this shortcoming, meaningful conclusions are drawn from the results.

spectrum. The personal attributes chosen were based on the existing literature (e.g. Broockman et al., 2021; Funk, 1996); surveys in Brazil focused on candidate attributes (e.g. Corrales et al., 2011); and conversations with public opinion scholars and political consultants. Gender emerged not only because of literature positing that voters punished female politicians more harshly for corruption (e.g. Anduiza et al., 2013; Esarey & Chirillo, 2013), but also because gender was an important difference between the two candidates in the field and survey experiment of previous field experimental work conducted by the author.

4.3 Estimation Strategy

Following the estimation approach described in Hainmueller, Hopkins, and Yamamoto (2014) and Hainmueller and Hopkins (2015), I estimate average marginal component effects (AMCEs). In this case, the AMCE represents the average difference in the probability of being preferred for voting when comparing two different values of an attribute, and allows for relative comparisons to be made across attributes. As an example, the AMCE comparing a candidate accused of accepting an illegal campaign contribution versus another accused of accepting a bribe for a government contract is an average effect that is taken over all possible combinations of the other candidate attributes. Because attributes are randomly assigned, the attributes of a candidate with the illegal campaign contribution will, on average, have the same distribution for all other attributes as the candidate accused of taking a bribe.

Specifically, each respondent, indexed by i, where $i \in \{1, \ldots, N\}$ is given k choice tasks, where $k \in \{1, 2, 3, 4\}$. For each task, the respondent, i, chooses the most preferred candidate between j possibilities, where $j \in \{1, 2\}$. The model estimated to obtain the AMCEs is an ordinary least squares (OLS) model of the following form:

$$
\begin{aligned}
Y_{ijk} = {}& \beta_0 + \beta_1 [\textit{Allegation}]_{ijk} + \beta_2 [\textit{Proceeding}]_{ijk} \\
& + \beta_3 [\textit{Abortion}]_{ijk} + \beta_4 [\textit{Juvenile Age}]_{ijk} \\
& + \beta_5 [\textit{Public Spending}]_{ijk} + \beta_6 [\textit{Party}]_{ijk} + \beta_7 [\textit{Gender}]_{ijk} \\
& + \beta_8 [\textit{Principal Characteristic}]_{ijk} + u_{ijk}
\end{aligned}
$$

Y_i is the outcome of interest, the candidate chosen by the respondent. Table 1 details the attributes and the respective baseline levels that are withheld in the specification and used as a reference category. Cluster-robust standard errors are clustered for each respondent, since the choices for each candidate pairing by an individual respondent are not independent. The specification has 9,600 observations, since the 1,200 respondents in the survey each completed 4 tasks involving a comparison of two candidates.[20]

Hainmueller et al. (2014) show that the estimator for the AMCEs is nonparametrically identified, and does not impose any functional form assumptions on the voter's utility function. While it has been common in the market research literature to estimate AMCEs with binary dependent variables using a conditional logit, Hainmueller et al. (2014) show that OLS provides unbiased estimates of the AMCEs.

One potential threat to the identification strategy is that respondents may not independently support the policy, but only choose the policy because the individual supports the party (Horiuchi et al., 2018). If respondents are doing this systematically, it would undermine the goal of isolating the effect of the voter's policy preference on their vote choice, since partisan attachment would be conflated with the policy preference.

While the possibility exists that respondents had strong partisan attachments and did not actually support the policies, a number of contextual factors mitigate this possibility. First, the programmatic content of party labels in Brazil is low relative to countries with institutionalized party systems, and even relative to other countries in Latin America. In 2014, the TSE reported that some 15.3 million of the country's 142.8 million voters were affiliated with parties. A nationally representative survey conducted in March 2016 by Datafolha, one of Brazil's leading polling firms, showed that only some 30 percent of the country had a preferred party.

Scholars have documented forces that cut against the importance of party labels in Brazil. Brazil has a newly formed party system; consequently, forces like parental socialization that are formative in countries like the United States are not nearly as important. Brazil also has one of the most highly fragmented party systems in the world (e.g. Figueiredo & Limongi, 2000; Kitschelt et al., 2010; Mainwaring, 1999); the large number of parties creates difficulties for the voter in discerning ideology among them. Moreover, institutions such as proportional electoral rules and open-list legislative elections increase difficulties for voters to understand party ideology and result in party coalitions that frequently change, undermining the brand that party labels can convey (Samuels & Zucco, 2014). Nevertheless, there is one party – the PT – where

---

[20] I had to link choices between corruption accusations and outcomes of judicial proceedings to avoid a combination where a candidate without corruption allegations was found guilty of corruption. For these linked outcomes, I followed Hainmueller et al. (2014) by using a generalized linear model (GLM) that included an interaction term with allegation and proceeding clustered by respondent. I then generated a weighted average treatment effect for every interaction of the treatment with other factors.

the label arguably is connected to policy positions. However, at the time that the conjoint experiment was conducted, the party was in flux with corruption scandals and the President's impeachment, resulting in ambiguity in the party's policies. Although the PT had a steady rise in individuals who identified with the party, reaching 25 percent by 2010, at the time that the conjoint experiment was launched, only 12 percent of respondents stated their preferred party was the PT. Thus, there is good reason to believe the experiment captures policy preferences of the respondents independent of their party preferences.

4.4 Results

I start by discussing the pooled results of the experiment.Results from a subgroup analysis that shows how the AMCEs differ based on voters' income follow the discussion of the pooled results.

4.4.1 Overall Results

Figure 3 shows the results for all candidate attributes for all respondents. Dots indicate the point estimates and lines show the 95 percent confidence intervals for the AMCE for each level within an attribute for the probability that

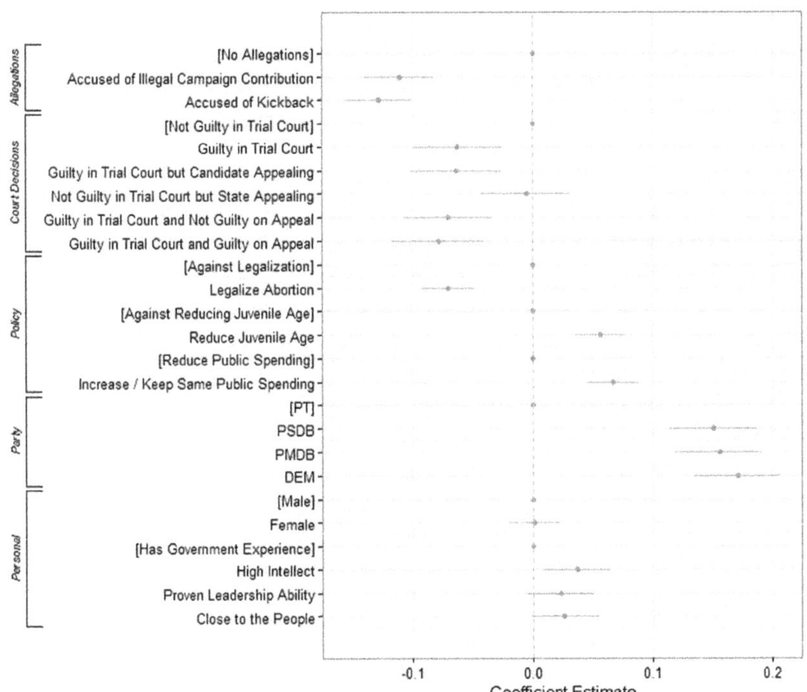

Figure 3 Effects of candidate attributes on vote choice

the respondents will choose a particular candidate. The baseline levels (also referred to as reference categories) are indicated with a dot without a line, and the variable name also appears in brackets. Following Hainmueller et al. (2014) and Hainmueller and Hopkins (2015), I include all of the pairwise interactions for linked attribute levels that impose restrictions on the randomization. For these AMCEs, I take the weighted average over the relevant attribute levels.

The point estimates first suggest that voters punish corruption and vote based on the type of corruption allegation. When the candidate is accused of accepting an illegal campaign contribution, the probability of winning a vote decreases by 11 percentage points (SE = 0.01) relative to a candidate with no corruption allegations. When the candidate is accused of accepting a kickback where there is private enrichment, the point estimate for the probability of winning a vote decreases to 12.8 percentage points (SE = 0.01), suggesting that voters are more repulsed by private enrichment forms of corruption. On one hand, the large effect that illegal campaign contributions would have in leading to the electoral punishment of a candidate is somewhat surprising, since field interviews with political consultants, polling experts, and political scientists in Brazil suggested that voters would be more tolerant of *caixa dois* (under-the-table campaign contributions). On the other hand, the salience of Rousseff's impeachment, along with the corruption of other politicians involved in *Lava Jato* and Petrobras scandals that were large-scale and prominent in the news at the time, likely increased the probability of voters punishing candidates for this type of corruption. Substantively, the results fall in line with the results of Botero et al. (2021, p. 16), who also find that private enrichment corruption is punished more harshly than clientelistic corruption.[21] This Element contrasts with that of scholars who claim that voters equate corruption across candidates or show that corruption is not that salient for voters (Almeida, 2008; Anderson & Tverdova, 2003; Chang & Golden, 2004; Rennó, 2007). Although the point estimates suggest that there is a difference, the differences between the two types of corruption are small and the confidence intervals are overlapping so we cannot rule out the possibility that voters do not distinguish between these types of corruption.

---

[21] Botero et al. (2021, p. 12) have a treatment condition where a clientelistic candidate "offer[ed] employment in public institutions and construction materials under the condition that [voters] would vote for him and participate in political events" and another candidate engaging in corruption for the purposes of private enrichment that misused public funds and could not justify a 450 percent increase in his wealth while he was in office. They found that private enrichment corruption reduced the candidate's support by 10 percentage points relative to the clientelistic candidate (Botero et al., 2021, p. 16).

Court decisions on corruption cases also have an important effect on corruption. If a candidate has only received a not guilty verdict at the trial court level and the decision is being appealed by the state, the case is not statistically distinguishable from the reference condition of the initial finding of not guilty without an appeal. This pattern suggests two important features in the responsiveness of voters to court decisions. First, even if a court found a candidate not guilty, one could imagine that voters might punish a candidate who was investigated by a prosecutor and who decided to pursue a trial. Second, voters may also distrust the courts, and think judges or the proof standards that have to be met, in large part, are established to let politicians off. Neither of these appears to be the case with these types of decisions in Brazil, which is somewhat surprising given the overall distrust in the state during the political context when this survey was completed. In all of the instances where a defendant had been judged not guilty (and had no other guilty verdict), the effect was not statistically distinguishable from zero. This lack of effect is also the case when the candidate is found not guilty, but the prosecution is appealing the decision (Estimate = −0.005, SE = 0.02). However, once there is a guilty verdict, whether or not it is being appealed or has been overturned, a candidate's chances of winning a vote decrease by between 6.2 and 7.8 percentage points (SE all equal 0.02). The results are consistent with voters not taking into account appellate decisions of acquittal, and with established proof standards making signals of guilt more trustworthy than signals of acquittal.

The policy positions taken by candidates all had an impact on the voter's decision. The baseline category for the three issues – abortion, age of majority for criminal responsibility, and fiscal spending – all involve the status quo at the time the survey was conducted. One pattern that is striking is that the magnitude of the AMCEs for the policy issues is roughly half of the magnitude of the impact of corruption allegations, but the magnitudes are in line with the impact of court decisions on corruption. A position favoring legalization of abortion, for example, reduces the probability of a vote by 7 percentage points (SE = 0.01), while support for reducing the criminal age of jurisdiction increases the probability of a vote by 5.7 percentage points (SE = 0.01). Support for expanding public spending increases one's vote probability by 6.3 percentage points (SE = 0.01). Although policy positions are often closely related to party, for reasons stated earlier I believe the context where this conjoint experiment was conducted gives good reason to believe that party preferences are independent of policy positions.

Political party had the greatest impact of any attribute on the respondent's vote choice. Point estimates for the three major parties – PSDB, PMDB, and DEM – relative to the PT were 15.0, 15.5, and 17.1 percentage points respectively (SEs = 0.02 for all three estimates). The difference relative to the PT is not surprising given the turmoil the party faced with corruption scandals and at the time the survey was conducted, a president facing impeachment. The strong results for the Democratic Party aligned with the most recent electoral trends prior to the survey favoring the right; in 2014, Brazilian voters elected the most conservative Congress in the last fifty years. However, in the October 2016 municipal elections, only 44.3 percent of mayors from the Democratic Party were reelected, relative to 53.1 and 47.3 percent for the PSDB and PMDB, respectively. The 2016 elections had a high combined rate of spoiled ballots and absenteeism (32.5 percent, up from 26.5 percent in 2012), so the possibility exists that a forced choice question may not account for possibilities of abstention and casting a spoiled ballot.

Turning to attributes, I find no support for the hypothesis that the candidate's gender leads to harsher or weaker willingness to vote for a female candidate, relative to similarly situated male candidates. The point estimate is 0.001 and the standard error is 0.01, so the results are small and not statistically significant ($p = 0.91$). The results contrast with the work of Teele et al. (2018), who find in conjoint experiments in the United States and work by other scholars in a number of other countries that voters respond favorably to female candidates. The results are in line with a number of studies showing that overt discrimination against female candidates is uncommon (e.g. Broockman et al., 2021; Lawless & Pearson, 2008; Teele et al., 2018). The conjoint experiment also included candidate attributes such as government experience, intellect, leadership ability, and being "close to the people." Having high intellect increased the probability of a vote by 3.7 percentage points (SE = 0.01). The remaining two attributes, closeness to the people and proven leadership ability, have similar effect sizes (2.7 and 2.3 percentage points, respectively). Though the standard errors are similar in size (SEs = 0.01) for the two attributes, the smaller magnitude of the coefficients lead them to be borderline in terms of conventional levels of statistical significance ($p = 0.07$ for closeness to the people, and $p = 0.11$ for proven leadership ability).

4.4.2 Results by Respondent Income

Moving to subgroup analysis, Figure 4 shows heterogeneity in preferences based on the respondent's level of income. Though Brazil has made significant strides to reduce income inequality in recent years, income inequality remains very high. The gap between the lowest and highest decile of income earners is five times as wide as in advanced economies (Samans et al., 2015). Consequently, the preferences for these two groups is likely to be distinct.

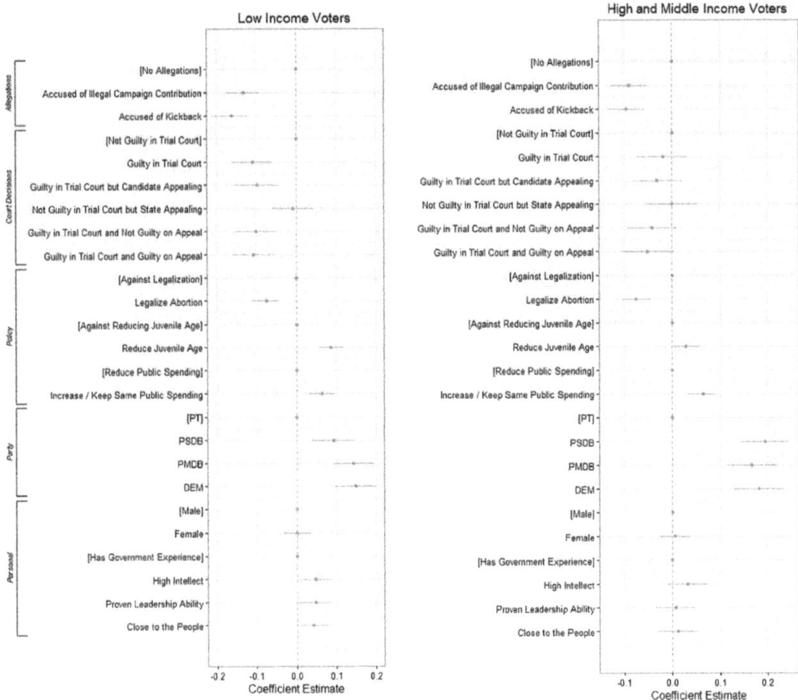

Figure 4 Effects of candidate attributes on vote choice by income

As was discussed earlier, one highly debated question in the literature relates to whether poor voters distinguish and punish based on corruption type.[22] The results show not only that the poor distinguish based on corruption type, but they are more likely to punish the candidate with corruption allegations. The poor are almost 1.5 times more likely to punish a candidate accused of accepting an illegal campaign contribution. The probability of punishment moves from 9.0 percent for the middle and high income respondents to 13.2 percent for the low income respondents (SEs are 0.02 for both subgroups). When a candidate engages in private enrichment, the poor are almost 1.7 times more likely to punish the candidate. The probability of punishment for the middle and high income respondents of 9.6 percent (SE = 0.02) jumps to 16.2 percent (SE = 0.02) for the poor respondents.

The poor are also more likely to punish the candidate based on court decisions. For middle and high income respondents, the probability of punishment was statistically distinguishable from 0 only in two situations when there was

---

[22] Lower income voters are defined as those in the lowest quintile of the income distribution. I use alternative cutoffs and the findings are substantively similar. Higher income voters are in the highest quintile of the income distribution.

an appeal. When the candidate received a guilty verdict that was overturned on appeal, middle and high income respondents were 5 percentage points less likely to vote for the candidate (SE = 0.03). When the candidate had been found guilty by a trial and appellate court and not guilty on appeal, the probability of a candidate's receiving a vote from the same respondents decreased by 4.1 percentage points (SE = 0.03). When the candidate had a guilty verdict and was in the process of appealing, the probability of the candidate receiving the vote of this subgroup decreased by 3.1 percentage points; this result, however, was close to the border of achieving statistical significance at conventional levels, but did not do so ($p = 0.12$). Poor respondents, by contrast, were responsive to all court decisions with a guilty verdict. The probability did not vary much according to the verdict; it ranged from -9.8 to -10.8 percent (all SEs = 0.03). The results suggest greater trust in the courts and prosecutors, a higher cynicism toward politicians found guilty at any stage of the court process, or some combination of those two possibilities for low-income voters. Middle- and high-income respondents, by contrast, need a very strong signal of guilt in order for their vote to be moved as a result of a court decision. The results are consistent with a view that middle- and higher-income respondents are only trusting of strong negative signals from courts, and otherwise vote on other dimensions, possibly because they are more distrusting of political parties and other institutions in dealing with corruption as Pavão (2018) and others have argued. By contrast, the poor are more willing to take into account a wider range of guilty signals from the court, and they do not change their preferences based on appeals or the actions of an appellate court.

The point estimates and confidence intervals were similar across policy positions and parties for both groups. The two exceptions were lowering the age of criminal responsibility and the PSDB party label. A candidate favoring a reduction of the age of majority increased the probability of a vote by 2.8 percentage points (SE = 0.02) for middle- and high-income respondents versus 8.6 percentage points (SE = 0.02) for the poor. The PSDB is a party known to be preferred by middle- and high-income voters. The PSDB party label increased the probability of a favorable vote from middle and high income respondents by 19.4 percentage points (SE = 0.03), more than twice that of poor respondents, whose probability of voting for a PSDB candidate increased by 9.3 percentage points (SE = 0.03). These results are relatively unsurprising, since the PSDB is known to have a stronger base among middle- and high-income voters (Samuels & Zucco, 2014).

Finally, with the exception of gender, income divided respondents in terms of their responsiveness to candidate attributes. The poor responded favorably to all three personal attributes of the candidates – high intellect, proven leadership, and closeness to the people. The probabilities of increasing their vote across the three attributes were similar; they ranged from 4.2 to 4.7 percentage points, and the SEs were all 0.02. This trend contrasted with wealthier respondents, who were not responsive to leadership or closeness of the candidate to the people (point estimates were 1.1 and 0.6 percentage points, but with SEs of 0.02, they were statistically indistinguishable from 0). The point estimate for intellect – the one attribute that had an effect in the pooled results – was higher at 3.1 percentage points, but with a p-value of 0.14, it did not achieve statistical significance at conventional levels.

5 Conclusion

Taken together, the framework and results of the conjoint experiment shed light on the mechanisms that lead voters to reward or punish corrupt politicians. All else equal, corruption accusations and court decisions on corruption diminish the probability of a candidate winning an election, but the effect of party labels outweighs the impact of the corruption allegation, irrespective of whether the allegation involved private enrichment or illegal campaign contributions. The effect of candidate party labels in combination with policy positions of the candidate and attributes also lead voters to reelect corrupt candidates. However, the effects of candidate policy positions and attributes are not enough for those factors alone to undermine the effects of corruption allegations and an adverse court proceeding involving corruption. Brazilian voters weigh policy positions of the candidate more heavily than their attributes, and I find no evidence that women are punished more harshly when they are accused or have proceedings involving corruption. One avenue for future research is to focus more prominently on the impact of voters' characteristics and on the potential interactions of other variables in the core specifications with the treatment.

A number of divergent trends emerge when comparing low income voters to middle and high income voters. Corruption allegations, irrespective of the type of corruption, have a similar effect in reducing the probability of a vote for a candidate, but middle and high income voters are much less responsive to court rulings on candidate corruption. The responsiveness of low income voters to court rulings suggest they are likely to be more trustworthy of courts in this instance. The contrasting results have implications for the trust that middle and high income voters place in the judiciary in these cases. The two groups are similar in how trade-offs are weighed with the policy positions of candidates, and party labels exert a stronger influence on middle and higher income voters. These trends not only stand in contrast to work that claims that the poor are not sensitive to corruption information (e.g. Almeida, 2008) and beliefs that they do not differentiate information from complex institutions such as courts. The stronger effects of party labels on middle and high income voters also shows how corruption scandals undermined the PT's stronger links with the poor. Finally, a contrast between the two income groups is seen – perhaps not surprisingly – in the higher responsiveness to attributes by low income voters.

The results have a number of implications for limiting corruption in the electoral arena. First, interventions targeting middle and high income voters that increase the legitimacy of courts in terms of their decision making in corruption cases would increase the salience and efficacy of corruption information in elections. Second, the high impact of party labels suggests the importance of placing less emphasis on candidate parties in disseminating corruption information. Finally, interventions targeting the poor should take into account the potential impact of candidate attributes that resonate with that population.

Appendix A
Survey Procedures

The survey was embedded within Ipsos Brasil's monthly omnibus survey, which included 1,200 face-to-face interviews conducted in 72 municipalities throughout Brazil in March and April of 2016. All interviews were audited to ensure the quality of responses. Our research team conducted the randomization, drafted the scripts for the conjoint portion of the survey, and attended training sessions given to the interviewers.

The sample was 52.2 percent female. Appendix B shows the distribution of other key variables in the survey.

Appendix B

Survey Sample: Descriptive Statistics

Table B1 Age distribution

Age range	*N*	Percent
16–24 years	230	19.17
25–34 years	281	23.42
35–44 years	239	19.92
45–59 years	286	23.83
60+ years	164	13.67
Total	1,200	100.00

Note: Mean age = 40 years; Median age = 38 years

Table B2 Education

Education level	*N*	Percent
Illiterate/Did not complete primary school	91	7.58
Completed primary school	104	8.67
Did not complete middle school	179	14.92
Completed middle school	183	15.25
Did not complete high school	117	9.75
Completed high school	317	26.42
Did not complete university	119	9.92
Completed university or more	90	7.50
Total	1,200	100.00

Table B3 Income level

Income level	*N*	Percent
A	22	1.83
B1	48	4
B2	239	19.92
C1	318	26.5
C2	313	26.08
D/E	260	21.67
Total	1,200	100.00

Table B4 Marital status

Marital status	*N*	Percent
Single	394	32.83
Married/domestic partnership	676	56.33
Separated	26	2.17
Divorced	48	4.00
Widowed	56	4.67
Total	1,200	100.00

Table B5 Location

Location	*N*	Percent
Capital	570	47.50
Interior	430	35.83
Metropolitan area	200	16.67
Total	1,200	100.00

Table B6 Distribution by state

State	*N*	Percent
Alagoas	20	1.67
Amazonas	50	4.17
Bahia	90	7.5
Ceará	40	3.33
Distrito Federal	40	3.33
Espiríto Santo	20	1.67
Goiás	20	1.67
Maranhão	30	2.5
Mato Grosso	20	1.67
Mato Grosso do Sul	20	1.67
Minas Gerais	100	8.33
Paraná	60	5
Paraíba	20	1.67
Pará	50	4.17
Pernambuco	40	3.33
Piauí	20	1.67

Table B6 Continued

State	*N*	Percent
Rio Grande do Norte	20	1.67
Rio Grande do Sul	70	5.83
Rio de Janeiro	120	10
Santa Catarina	30	2.5
Sergipe	10	0.83
São Paulo	310	25.83
Total	1,200	100.00

Table B7 Distribution by region

Region	*N*	Percent
Center-West	100	8.33
Northeast	290	24.17
North	100	8.33
Southeast	550	45.83
South	160	13.33
Total	1,200	100.00

Appendix C
Additional Results

Table C1 Effects of candidate attributes on vote choice

Attribute	Coefficient	SE	*p*-value
Accused of illegal campaign contribution	−0.110	0.014	0.001
Accused of kickback	−0.128	0.014	0.000
Guilty in trial court	−0.062	0.019	0.001
Guilty in trial court but candidate appealing	−0.064	0.019	0.000
Not guilty in trial court but state appealing	−0.005	0.019	0.400
Guilty in trial court and not guilty on appeal	−0.070	0.019	0.000
Guilty in trial court and guilty on appeal	−0.078	0.019	0.000
Legalize abortion	−0.070	0.011	0.000
Reduce juvenile age	0.057	0.011	0.000
Increase/Keep same public spending	0.067	0.011	0.000
PSDB	0.150	0.019	0.000
PMDB	0.155	0.019	0.000
DEM	0.171	0.018	0.000
Female	0.001	0.011	0.911
High intellect	0.037	0.014	0.009
Proven leadership ability	0.023	0.014	0.108
Close to the people	0.027	0.014	0.065

Table C2 Effects of candidate attributes on vote choice - low-income voters

Attribute	Coefficient	SE	*p*-value
Accused of illegal campaign contribution	−0.132	0.022	0.000
Accused of Kickback	−0.162	0.022	0.000
Guilty in trial court	−0.108	0.026	0.000
Guilty in trial court but candidate appealing	−0.098	0.027	0.000
Not guilty in trial court but state appealing	−0.008	0.026	0.378
Guilty in trial court and not guilty on appeal	−0.101	0.027	0.000
Guilty in trial court and guilty on appeal	−0.107	0.027	0.000
Legalize abortion	−0.075	0.017	0.000
Reduce juvenile age	0.086	0.016	0.000

Table C2 Continued

Attribute	Coefficient	SE	*p*-value
Increase/keep same public spending	0.064	0.016	0.000
PSDB	0.093	0.028	0.001
PMDB	0.144	0.027	0.000
DEM	0.149	0.027	0.000
Female	0.001	0.017	0.940
High intellect	0.047	0.022	0.030
Proven leadership ability	0.047	0.021	0.026
Close to the people	0.042	0.021	0.052

Table C3 Effects of candidate attributes on vote choice - middle- & high-income voters

Attribute	Coefficient	SE	*p*-value
Accused of illegal campaign contribution	−0.090	0.020	0.000
Accused of kickback	−0.096	0.020	0.000
Guilty in trial court	−0.019	0.027	0.241
Guilty in trial court but candidate appealing	−0.031	0.027	0.123
Not Guilty in trial court but state appealing	0.000	0.027	0.504
Guilty in trial court and not guilty on appeal	−0.041	0.026	0.058
Guilty in trial court and guilty on appeal	−0.052	0.028	0.034
Legalize abortion	−0.074	0.016	0.000
Reduce juvenile age	0.028	0.016	0.076
Increase/keep same public spending	0.064	0.015	0.000
PSDB	0.194	0.026	0.000
PMDB	0.166	0.027	0.000
DEM	0.182	0.027	0.000
Female	0.006	0.016	0.716
High intellect	0.031	0.021	0.144
Proven leadership ability	0.007	0.022	0.757
Close to the people	0.011	0.021	0.588

References

Achen, C. H. (2016). Grupo protesta em SP contra Temer e a favor de Dilma. *Globo*. http://g1.globo.com/sao-paulo/noticia/2016/05/grupo-protesta-em-sp-contra-presidente-em-exercicio-michel-temer.html.

Achen, C. H. (2002). Parental Socialization and Rational Party Identification. *Political Behavior*, *24*(2), 151–170.

Adserà, A., Boix, C., & Payne, M. (2003). Are You Being Served? Political Accountability and Quality of Government. *Journal of Law, Economics and Organization*, *19*(2), 445–490.

Aguilar, R. et al. (2015). Ballot Structure, Candidate Race, and Vote Choice in Brazil. *Latin American Research Review*, *50*(3), 175–202.

Almeida, A. C. (2008). *A cabeça do eleitor: Estratégia de campanha, pesquisa e vitória eleitoral*. Editor Record.

Alvarez, R. M. (1998). *Information and Elections*. Ann Arbor, MI: University of Michigan Press.

Anderson, C. J., & Tverdova, Y. V. (2003). Corruption, Political Allegiances, and Attitudes toward Government in Contemporary Democracies. *American Journal of Political Science*, *47*(1), 91–109.

Anduiza, E., Gallego, A., & Muñoz, J. (2013, February). Turning a Blind Eye: Experimental Evidence of Partisan Bias in Attitudes toward Corruption. *Comparative Political Studies*, *46*(12), 1664–1692. Retrieved 2021-03-09, http://journals.sagepub.com/doi/10.1177/0010414013489081.

Ansolabehere, S., & Snyder Jr., J. M. (2000). Valence Politics and Equilibrium in Spatial Election Models. *Public Choice*, *103*(3/4), 327–336.

Arceneaux, K. (2007). I'm Asking for Your Support: The Effects of Personally Delivered Campaign Messages on Voting Decisions and Opinion Formation. *Quarterly Journal of Political Science*, *2*(1), 43–65.

Auyero, J. (2001). *Poor People's Politics: Peronist Survival Networks and the Legacy of Evita*. Durham, NC: Duke University Press.

Bardhan, P. (1997). Corruption and Development: A Review of Issues. *Journal of Economic Literature*, *35*(3), 1320–1346. www.jstor.org/stable/2729979.

Banerjee, A., Green, D., Green, J., & Pande, R. (2010). Can Voters be Primed to Choose Better Legislators? Experimental Evidence from Rural India. Working Paper 105.

Banerjee, A. V., Kumar, S., Pande, R., & Su, F. (2011). Do Informed Voters Make Better Choices? Experimental Evidence from Urban India. Working Paper 142.

Barros, L., Goldszmidt, R., & Pereira, C. (2019). Why Do Voters Choose Corrupt Candidates? The Role of Ideology on Cognitive Mechanisms. *International Journal of Public Opinion Research*, (edz041), 1–18.

Bartolini, S., & Mair, P. (1990). *Identity, Competition and Electoral Availability: The Stabilisation of European Electorates, 1885–1985*. New York: Cambridge University Press.

Bauhr, M. & Grimes, M. (2014). Indignation or Resignation: The Implications of Transparency for Societal Accountability. *Governance, 27*(2), 291–320.

Besley, T., & Burgess, R. (2002). The Political Economy of Government Responsiveness: Theory and Evidence from India. *Quarterly Journal of Economics, 117*(4), 1415–1451.

Besley, T., & Prat, A. (2006). Handcuffs for the Grabbing Hand? The Role of the Media in Political Accountability. *American Economic Review, 96*(3), 720–736.

Black, D. (1958). *The Theory of Committees and Elections*. New York: Cambridge University Press.

Botero, S., Cornejo, R. C., Gamboa, L., Pavão, N., & Nickerson, D. W. (2015). Says Who? An Experiment on Allegations of Corruption and Credibility of Sources. *Political Research Quarterly, 68*(3), 493–504. www.jstor.org/stable/24637789.

Botero, S., Cornejo, R. C., Gamboa, L., Pavão, N., & Nickerson, D. W. (2021). Are All Types of Corruption Created Equal in the Eyes of Voters? *Journal of Elections, Public Opinion and Parties, 31*(2), 141–158. https://doi.org/10.1080/17457289.2019.1651322

Broockman, D. E., Carnes, N., Crowder-Meyer, M., & Skovron, C. (2021). Why Local Party Leaders Don't Support Nominating Centrists. *British Journal of Political Science, 51*(2), 724–749. doi:10.1017/S0007123419000309

Brooks, D. J. & Murov, M. (2012). Assessing Accountability in a Post-Citizens United Era: The Effects of Attack Ad Sponsorship by Unknown Independent Groups. *American Politics Research, 40*(3), 383–418. https://doi.org/10.1177/1532673X11414791.

Brunetti, A., & Weder, B. (2003). A Free Press Is Bad News for Corruption. *Journal of Public Economics, 87*(7), 1801–1824.

Bucureasa, C. (2016). Romanian Mayors Re-Elected Despite Corruption Probes. *Balkan Insight*. www.balkaninsight.com/en/article/romanian-politicians-investigated-for-corruption-re-elected-mayors-06-06-2016.

Bullock, J. G. (2011). Elite Influence on Public Opinion in an Informed Electorate. *American Political Science Review, 105*(3), 496–515.

Cain, B. E., Ferejohn, J. A., & Fiorina, M. P. (1987). *The Personal Vote: Constituency Service and Electoral Independence*. Cambridge, MA: Harvard University Press.

Campbell, A., Converse, P. E., Miller, W. E., & Stokes, D. E. (1960). *The American Voter*. New York. The University of Chicago Press.

Chang, E. C. C., & Golden, M. A. (2004). Does Corruption Pay? The Survival of Politicians Changed with Malfeasance in the Postwar Intalian Chamber of Deputies. Working Paper, paper presented at the Annual Meeting of the American Political Science Association, Chicago, September 2–5.

Chang, E. C. C., & Golden, M. A. (2007). Electoral Systems, District Magnitude and Corruption. *British Journal of Political Science, 37*(1), 115–137.

Chayes, S. (2018). Fighting the Hydra: Lessons Learned from Worldwide Protests against Corruption. https://carnegieendowment.org/2018/04/12/ fighting-hydra-lessons-from-worldwide-rotests-against-corruption-pub-760 36.

Chong, A., De La O, A. L., Karlan, D., & Wantchekon, L. (2015). Does Corruption Information Inspire the Fight or Quash the Hope? A Field Experiment in Mexico on Voter Turnout, Choice, and Party Identification. *Journal of Politics, 77*(1), 55–71.

Clark, M. (2009). Valence and Electoral Outcomes in Western Europe, 1976– 1998. *Electoral Studies, 28*(1), 111–122.

Converse, P. E. (1969). Of Time and Partisan Stability. *Comparative Political Studies, 2*(2), 139–171.

Corrales, B., Adrogué, G., & Armesto, M. (2011). 'Você decide!' Usando a Conjoint Analysis para entender o voto dos eleitores do Brasil e Argentina. Working Paper, paper presented at the 4th congresso Latino americano de Opinião Pública da Wapor.

Craig, S., Rashbaum, W. K., & Kaplan, T. (2016). The Many Faces of New York's Political Scandals. *New York Times*.

Curini, L. (2015). The Conditional Ideological Inducement to Campaign on Character Valence Issues in Multiparty Systems: The Case of Corruption. *Comparative Political Studies, 48*(2), 168–192.

Curini, L., & Martelli, P. (2010). Ideological Proximity and Valence Competition: Negative Campaigning through Allegation of Corruption in the Italian Legislative Arena from 1946 to 1994. *Electoral Studies, 29*(4), 636–647.

Dahl, R. A. (1973). Polyarchy: Participation and Opposition. New Haven, CT: Yale University Press.

Dahl, R. A. (1989). Democracy and Its Critics. New Haven, CT: Yale University Press.

de Figueiredo, M. F. P., Hidalgo, F. D., & Kasahara, Y. (2023). When Do Voters Punish Corrupt Politicians? Experimental Evidence from a Field and Survey Experiment. *British Journal of Political Science, 53*(2), 728–739. https://doi.org/10.1017/S0007123421000727.

de Sousa, L., & Moriconi, M. (2013). Why Voters Do Not Throw the Rascals Out? A Conceptual Framework for Analysing Electoral Punishment of Corruption. *Crime, Law and Social Change, 60*(5), 471–502.

Dewan, T., & Shepsle, K. (2011). Political Economy Models of Elections. *Annual Review of Political Science, 14,* 311–330.

Dickson, E. S., Gordon, S.C. & Huber G. A. (2015). Institutional Sources of Legitimate Authority: An Experimental Investigation. *American Journal of Political Science, 59,* 109–127.

Domingo, P. (2004). Judicialization of Politics or Politicization of the Judiciary? Recent Trends in Latin America. *Democratization, 11*(1), 104–126.

Downs, A. (1957). *An Economic Theory of Democracy.* New York: Harper and Row.

Dunning, T. et al. (eds.) 2019, *Information, Accountability, and Cumulative Learning: Lessons from Metaketa I.* Cambridge University Press, Cambridge Studies in Comparative Politics.

Esarey, J., & Chirillo, G. (2013). "Fairer Sex" or Purity Myth? Corruption, Gender and Institutional Context. *Politics and Gender, 9,* 361–389.

Feddersen, T. J., & Pesendorfer, W. (1996). The Swing Voter's Curse. *American Economic Review, 86*(3), 408–424.

Ferejohn, J. (2002). Judicializing Politics, Politicizing Law. *Law and Contemporary Problems, 65*(3), 41–68. www.jstor.org/stable/1192402?origin= crossref, https://doi.org/10.2307/1192402.

Ferraz, C., & Finan, F. (2008). Exposing Corrupt Politicians: The Effects of Brazil's Publicly Released Audits on Electoral Outcomes. *Quarterly Journal of Economics, 123*(2), 703–745.

Figueiredo, A. C., & Limongi, F. (2000). Presidential Power, Legislative Organization, and Party Behavior in Brazil. *Comparative Politics, 32*(2), 151–170.

Fowler, E. F. & Ridout, T. N. (2009). Local Television and Newspaper Coverage of Advertising. *Political Communication, 26,* 119–136.

Fiorina, M. P. (1981). *Retrospective Voting in American National Elections.* New Haven, CT: Yale University Press.

Funk, C. L. (1996). The Impact of Scandal on Candidate Evaluations: An Experi- mental Test of the Role of Candidate Traits. *Political Behavior, 18*(1), 1–24.

Fávero, B. (2016). Movimentos feministas fazem ato anti-Cunha e pró-Dilma em São Paulo. *Folha de São Paulo.* www1.folha.uol.com.br/poder/2016/03/1747762-movimentos-feministas-fazem-ato-anti-cunha-e-pro-dilma-em-sao-paulo.shtml.

Gallie, W. B. (1956). Essentially Contested Concepts. In Proceedings of the Aristotelian Society 56, pp. 167–198.

Gans-Morse, J., Mazzuca, S. & Nichter, S. (2014). Varieties of Clientelism: Machine Politics during Elections. *American Journal of Political Science, 58*(2), 415–432.

Gingerich, D. W. (2009). Corruption and Political Decay: Evidence from Bolivia. *Quarterly Journal of Political Science, 4*(1), 1–34.

Gordon, S. C. (2009). Assessing Partisan Bias in Federal Public Corruption Prosecutions. *American Political Science Review, 103*(4), 534–554.

Gordon, S. C. & Huber, G. A. (2009). The Political Economy of Prosecution. *Annual Review of Law and Social Science, 5*, 135–156.

Green, J. (2007). When Voters and Parties Agree: Valence Issues and Party Competition. *Political Studies, 55*(3), 629–655.

Green, D. P., Palmquist, B., & Schickler, E. (2002). *Partisan Hearts and Minds: Political Parties and the Social Identities of Voters*. New Haven, CT: Yale University Press.

Guerriero, C. (2020). Endogenous Institutions and Economic Outcomes. *Economica*, 87, 364–405.

Hainmueller, J., & Hopkins, D. J. (2015). The Hidden American Immigration Consensus: A Conjoint Analysis of Attitudes toward Immigrants. *American Journal of Political Science, 59*(3), 529–548.

Hainmueller, J., Hopkins, D. J., & Yamamoto, T. (2014). Causal Inference in Conjoint Analysis: Understanding Multidimensional Choices via Stated Preference Experiments. *Political Analysis, 22*(1), 1–30.

Hayes, D. (2005). Candidate Qualities through a Partisan Lens: A Theory of Trait Ownership. *American Journal of Political Science, 49*(4), 908–923.

Helmke, G., & Levitsky, S. (2004). Informal Institutions and Comparative Politics: A Research Agenda. *Perspectives on Politics, 2*(4), 725–740. www.jstor.org/stable/3688540.

Horiuchi, Y., Smith, D. M., & Yamamoto, T. (2018). Measuring Voters' Multidimensional Policy Preferences with Conjoint Analysis: Application to Japan's 2014 Election. *Political Analysis, 26*(2), 190–209.

Hotelling, H. (1929). Stability in Competition. *Economic Journal, 39*(153), 41–57.

Humphreys, M., & Weinstein, J. M. (2012). Policing Politicians: Citizen Empowerment and Accountability in Uganda – Preliminary Analysis. Working Paper, unpublished.

Jackson, M., & Smith, R. (1996). Inside Moves and Outside Views: An Australian Case Study of Elite and Public Perceptions of Political Corruption. *Governance, 9*(1), 23–42.

Jackman, S., & Sniderman. P. M. (2002). Institutional Organization of Choice Spaces: A Political Conception of Political Psychology. In K. R. Monroe (Eds.), *Political Psychology* (pp. 209–225). Mahwah, NJ: Lawrence Erlbaum Associates Publishers.

Jana, K. & Rose-Ackerman. S. (2005). Electoral Rules and Constitutional Structures as Constraints on Corruption. *British Journal of Political Science, 35*(4), 573–606.

Jennings, M. K., & Niemi, R. G. (1981). *Generations and Politics*. Princeton, NJ: Princeton University Press.

Key Jr., V. O. (1966). *The Responsible Electorate Rationality in Presidential Voting 1936–1960*. Cambridge, MA: Harvard University Press.

Kitschelt, H., Hawkins, K. A., Luna, J. P., Rosas, G., & Zechmeister, E. J. (2010). *Latin American Party Systems*. New York: Cambridge University Press.

Kinder, D. R. (1986). Presidential character revisited. In R. R. Lau and D. O. Sears (Eds.), *Political Cognition* (pp. 233–255). Hillsdale, NJ: Erlbaum.

Klašjna, M., & Tucker, J. A. (2013). The Economy, Corruption, and the Vote: Evidence from Experiments in Sweden and Moldova. *Electoral Studies, 32*, 536–543.

Klašjna, M., Tucker, J. A., & Deegan–Krause, K. (2016). Pocketbook vs Sociotropic Corruption Voting. *British Journal of Political Science, 46*(1), 67–94.

Klašnja, M., Lupu, N., & Tucker, J. A. (2021). When Do Voters Sanction Corrupt Politicians? *Journal of Experimental Political Science*, 8(2),161-171. doi:10.1017/XPS.2020.13, https://doi.org/10.1017/XPS.2020.13.

Kunicova, J. & Rose-Ackerman, S. (2005). Electoral Rules and Constitutional Structures as Constraints on Corruption. *British Journal of Political Science, 35*(4), 573–606.

Kurer, O. (2005). Corruption: An Alternative Approach to Its Definition and Measurement. *Political Studies, 53*(1), 222–239.

Lawless, J. L., & Pearson, K. (2008). The Primary Reason for Women's Underrepresentation? Reevaluating the Conventional Wisdom. *Journal of Politics, 70*(1), 67–82.

Levitsky, S. (2003). *Transforming Labor-Based Parties in Latin America*. New York: Cambridge University Press.

Lupia, A., & McCubbins, M. D. (1998). *The democratic dilemma: Can citizens learn what they need to know?* New York: Cambridge University Press.

Mainwaring, S. (1999). *Rethinking Party Systems in the Third Wave of Democratization: The Case of Brazil*. Stanford, CA: Stanford University Press.

Mainwaring, S., & Torcal, M. (2006). Party System Institutionalization and Party System Theory after the Third Wave of Democratization. In R. S. Katz & W. Crotty (Eds.), *Handbook of Political Parties* (pp. 204–227). London: Sage.

Malesky, E., Schuler, P., & Tran, A. (2012). The Adverse Effects of Sunshine: A Field Experiment on Legislative Transparency in an Authoritarian Assembly. *American Political Science Review, 106*(4), 762–786.

Malhotra, N., & Kuo, A. G. (2008). Attributing Blame: The Public's Response to Hurricane Katrina. *Journal of Politics, 70*(1), 120–135.

Mancuso, M. et al. (1998). *A Question of Ethics: Canadians Speak Out*. New York: Oxford University Press.

Markus, G. B. (1982). Political Attitudes during an Election Year: A Report on the 1980 NES Panel Study. *American Political Science Review, 76*(3), 538–560.

Miller, W. E., & Shanks, J. M. (1996). *The New American Voter*. Cambridge, MA: Harvard University Press.

McCann, J. A., & Dominguez, J. I. (1998). Mexicans React to Electoral Fraud and Political Corruption: An Assessment of Public Opinion and Voting Behavior. *Electoral Studies, 17*(4), 483–503.

McCann, J. A., & Lawson, C. (2003). An Electorate Adrift? Public Opinion and the Quality of Democracy in Mexico. *Latin American Research Review, 38*(3), 60–81.

Myerson, R. B. (1993). Effectiveness of Electoral Systems for Reducing Government Corruption: A Game-Theoretic Analysis. *Games and Economic Behavior, 5*(1), 118–132.

Nannicini, T., Stella A., Tabellini, G., & Troiano, U. (2013). Social Capital and Political Accountability. *American Economic Journal: Economic Policy, 5*(2), 222–250. www.aeaweb.org/articles?id=10.1257/pol.5.2.222.

North, D. C. (1990). *Institutions, Institutional Change, and Economic Performance*. New York: Cambridge University Press.

Nye, Joseph S. (1967). Corruption and Political Development: A Cost-Benefit Analysis. *American Political Science Review, 61*(2), 417–427.

McCullough, A. (2015). *The Legitimacy of States and Armed Non-State Actors* (Tech. Rep.). Birmingham: University of Birmingham.

Palfrey, T. R., & Poole, K. T. (1987). The Relationship between Information, Ideology, and Voting Behavior. *American Journal of Political Science, 31*(3), 511–530.

Pande, R. (2011). Can Informed Voters Enforce Better Governance? Experiments in Low Income Democracies. *Annual Review of Economics, 3*, 215–237.

Pavão, N. (2018). Corruption as the Only Option: The Limits to Electoral Accountability. *Journal of Politics, 80*(3), 996–1010.

Pavão, N. (2019). Corruption, Courts, and Public Opinion in Brazil. In Robert I. Rotberg (Ed), *Corruption in Latin America: How Politicians and Corporations Steal from Citizens* (pp. 93–107). New York: Springer.

Pereira, C., Melo, M. A., & Figueiredo, C. M. (2009). The Corruption-Enhancing Role of Re-election Incentives? Counterintuitive Evidence from Brazil's Audit Reports. *Political Research Quarterly, 62*(4), 731–744.

Persson, T., Tabellini, G., & Trebbi, F. (2003). Electoral Rules and Corruption. *Journal of the European Economic Association, 1*(4), 958–989.

Peters, J., & Welch, S. (1980). The Effects of Charges of Corruption on Voting Behavior in Congressional Elections. *American Political Science Review, 74*(3), 697–708.

Pitkin, H. F. (1967). *The Concept of Representation*. Berkeley, CA: University of California Press.

Powell, G. B. (2007). Aggregating and Representing Political Preferences. In C. Boix & S. C. Stokes (Eds.), *Oxford Handbook of Comparative Politics* (pp. 653–677). New York: Oxford University Press.

Power, T. J., & Taylor, M. M. (2011). *Corruption and Democracy in Brazil: The Struggle for Accountability*. Notre Dame, IN: University of Notre Dame Press.

Przeworski, A. (2003). Freedom to Choose and Democracy. *Economics and Philosophy, 19*, 265–279. https://doi.org/10.1017/S0266267103001159.

Przeworski, A., Stokes, S. C., B. (Eds.). (1999). *Democracy, Accountability, and Representation*. New York: Cambridge University Press.

Rennó, L. R. (2007). Escândalos e voto: As eleições presidenciais brasileiras de 2006. *Opinião Pública, 13*(2), 260–282.

Rundquist, B. S., Strom, G. S., & Peters, J. G. (1977). Corrupt Politicians and Their Electoral Support: Some Experimental Observations. *American Political Science Review, 71*(3), 954–963.

Samans, R., Blanke, J., Corrigan, G., & Drzeniek, M. (2015). *Is Brazil Making Progress on Inequality?* (Tech. Rep.). www.weforum.org/agenda/2015/09/is-brazil-making-progress-on-inequality.

Samuels, D. J. (2006). Sources of Mass Partisanship in Brazil. *Latin American Politics and Society*, *48*(2), 1–27.

Samuels, D. J., & Zucco, C. (2014). The Power of Partisanship in Brazil: Evidence from Survey Experiments. *American Journal of Political Science*, *58*(1), 212–225.

Scott, J. C. (1972). *Comparative Political Corruption*. Upper Saddle River, NJ: Prentice-Hall.

Sieder, R., Schjolden, L., & Angell, A. (2005). *The Judicialization of Politics in Latin America*. New York: Palgrave Macmillan.

Slomczynski, K. M., & Shabad, G. (2012). Perceptions of Political Party Corruption and Voting Behaviour in Poland. *Party Politics*, 18, 896–917.

Smith, S. (2016). Brazil's Congress – A Den of Corruption. *Agence France Presse (AFP)*. www.yahoo.com/news/brazils-congress-den-corruption-1730 41998.html.

Stephenson, M. C. (2015). Corruption and Democratic Institutions: A Review and Synthesis, In Susan Rose-Ackerman & Paul Lagunes (eds.), *Greed, Corruption, and the Modern State*, Cheltenham, UK: Edward Elgar Publishing. pp. 92–133.

Stokes, D. E. (1963). Spatial Models of Party Competition. *American Political Science Review*, *57*(2), 368–377.

Stone Sweet, A. (2000). *Governing with Judges: Constitutional Politics in Europe*. New York: Oxford University Press.

Stokes, Susan C. et al. (2013). *Brokers, Voters, and Clientelism: The Puzzle of Distributive Politics*. New York: Cambridge University Press.

Szwarcberg, M. (2012). Uncertainty, Political Clientelism, and Voter Turnout in Latin America: Why Parties Conduct Rallies in Argentina. *Comparative Politics*, *45*(1), 88–106.

Teele, D. L., Kalla, J., & Rosenbluth, F. (2018). The Ties that Double Bind: Social Roles and Women's Underrepresentation in Politics. *American Political Science Review*, *112*(3), 525–541.

Treisman, D. (2000). The Causes of Corruption: A Cross-National Study. *Journal of Public Economics*, *76*(3), 399–457.

Truex, R. (2011). Corruption, Attitudes, and Education: Survey Evidence from Nepal. *World Development*, *39*(7), 1133–1142.

Varghese, J. (2014). 186 Indian Members of Parliament Have Criminal Cases Including Murder and Rape. *International Business Times*. www.ibtimes.co.in/186-indian-members-parliament-have-criminal-cases-including-murder-rape-600584.

Weitz-Shapiro, R., & Winters, M. S. (2017). Can Citizens Discern? Information, Credibility, Sophistication, and the Punishment of Corruption in Brazil. *Journal of Politics, 79*(1), 60–74.

Welch, S., & Hibbing, J. R. (1997). The Effects of Charges of Corruption on Voting Behavior in Congressional Elections, 1982–1990. *Journal of Politics, 59*(1), 226–239.

Weschle, S. (2016). Punishing Personal and Electoral Corruption: Experimental Evidence from India. *Research and Politics, 3*(2), 1–6.

Wesleyan Media Project. (2016). Eschewing Policy in Advertising? Lessons from 2016. Middletown, CT: Wesleyan Media Project Press.

Winters, M. S., & Weitz–Shapiro, R. (2013). Lacking Information or Con- doning Corruption: When Do Voters Support Corrupt Politicians? *Comparative Politics, 45*(4), 418–436.

Winters, M. S., & Weitz–Shapiro, R. (2015). Political Corruption and Partisan Engagement: Evidence from Brazil. *Journal of Politics in Latin America, 7*(1), 45–81.

Wolfinger, R. E., & Rosenstone, S. J. (1980). *Who Votes?* New Haven, CT: Yale University Press.

Zaller, J. (1992). *The Nature and Origin of Mass Opinion.* New York: Cambridge University Press.

Zarazaga, R. (2014). Brokers Beyond Clientelism: A New Perspective Through the Argentine Case. *Latin American Politics and Society, 56*(3), 23–45.

Acknowledgments

I thank Jill Anderson, Diego Werneck Arguelhes, George Avelino, Ciro Biderman, Henry Brady, Gabriel Cepaluni, Paulo Furquim de Azevedo, Thad Dunning, Carmine Guerriero, Ivar Hartmann, Danny Hidalgo, Ben Johnson, Jed Kroncke, Yuri Kasahara, Fernando Limongi, Marcus Melo, Dan Mattingly, Lindsay Mayka, Lucas Novaes, Nara Pavão, Mariana Mota Prado, J.J. Prescott, Leonardo Rosa, Peter Siegelman, Doug Spencer, Richard A. Wilson, Matt Winters, the editors and anonymous reviewers from the *Cambridge Elements in Law, Economics and Politics* series, and participants at the Canadian Law & Economics Association (CLEA) Annual Meeting at the University of Toronto, the Society for the Advancement of Socio-Economics (SASE) Conference in Lyon, France, and at Insper Law School's faculty workshop in São Paulo for helpful feedback. Martina Bergues, Natalia Maia, Thiago Nascimento da Silva, and Sergio Simoni Junior provided helpful research assistance. I am also grateful to Fernando Limongi and the National Science Foundation for providing financial support for this project. Finally, I am most grateful to my family. My wife, Margaret Boittin, has been a source of incredible support and insight from the very beginning of this project. She also gave of her time – including caring for our children, watching our household, and taking away time from her own research – which made the completion of this work possible. My parents, Rui de Figueiredo, Sr. and Isabel de Figueiredo, and my siblings, Alcina Dalton, Paul de Figueiredo, John de Figueiredo, and Rui de Figueiredo, Jr., and their spouses, James Dalton, Kathy de Figueiredo, Bronwyn de Figueiredo, and Natalia Ferretti have all been incredible sources of strength and support through my highest and lowest moments and continue to keep me going.

Cambridge Elements

Law, Economics and Politics

Series Editor in Chief
Carmine Guerriero, *University of Bologna*

Series Co-Editors
Alessandro Riboni, *École Polytechnique*
Jillian Grennan, *Duke University, Fuqua School of Business*
Petros Sekeris, *TBS Education*

Series Managing Editor
Valentino Moscariello, *University of Bologna*

Series Associate Editors
Maija Halonen-Akatwijuka, *University of Bristol*
Sara Biancini, *Université de Cergy-Pontoise*
Melanie Meng Xue, *London School of Economics and Political Science*
Claire Lim, *Queen Mary University of London*
Andy Hanssen, *Clemson University*
Giacomo Benati, *Eberhard Karls University, Tübingen*

About the Series
Decisions taken by individuals are influenced by formal and informal institutions. Legal and political institutions determine the nature, scope and operation of markets, organisations and states. This interdisciplinary series analyses the functioning, determinants, and impact of these institutions, organizing the existing knowledge and guiding future research.

For EU product safety concerns, contact us at Calle de José Abascal, 56–1°,
28003 Madrid, Spain or eugpsr@cambridge.org.

www.ingramcontent.com/pod-product-compliance
Ingram Content Group UK Ltd.
Pitfield, Milton Keynes, MK11 3LW, UK
UKHW030806150425
457293UK00016B/211